Guide to Negotiable Instrume
Exchange Acts

Guide to
Negotiable Instruments
and the
Bills of Exchange Acts

Seventh edition

Dudley Richardson
BSc (Econ) Lond, AIB, AMBIM, Dip E & T of Institute of Bankers

London
Butterworths
1983

England	Butterworth & Co (Publishers) Ltd 88 Kingsway, London WC2B 6AB
Australia	Butterworths Pty Ltd 271–273 Lane Cove Road, North Ryde, NSW 2113 Also at Melbourne, Brisbane, Adelaide and Perth
Canada	Butterworth & Co (Canada) Ltd 2265 Midland Avenue, Scarborough, Ont M1P 4S1
	Butterworth & Co (Western Canada) Ltd 409 Granville Street, Ste 856, Vancouver, BC V6C 1T2
New Zealand	Butterworths of New Zealand Ltd 33–35 Cumberland Place, Wellington
Singapore	Butterworth & Co (Asia) Pte Ltd Crawford Post Office Box 770 Singapore 9119
South Africa	Butterworth & Co (South Africa) (Pty) Ltd Box No 792, Durban
United States of America	Mason Publishing Company Finch Building, 366 Wacouta Street, St Paul, Minn 55101
	Butterworth (Legal Publishers) Inc 160 Roy Street, Ste 300, Seattle, Wash 98109
	Butterworth (Legal Publishers) Inc 381 Elliot Street, Newton, Upper Falls, Mass 02164

© Butterworth & Co (Publishers) Ltd 1983

ISBN 0 406 64824 7

Typeset by Phoenix Photosetting, Chatham
Printed and bound by Biddles Ltd, Guildford and King's Lynn

Preface to the seventh edition

A fresh edition of the book has enabled me to make a few but necessary additions and alterations as a result of the abolition of the Business-Names Register (Companies Act 1981). Further, I have made brief references to the *Marfini* case and the *Lumsden* case under section 4 of the Cheques Act since the courts have emphasised now that the taking up of references from strangers opening new current accounts should be more than a formality. The *Lumsden* case brought with its judgment a very exceptional view of section 64 of the 1882 Act which I have recorded.

I have added a small chapter at the end of the book on the modern development of Bankers Cards and Cheque Cards so as to avoid any confusion of such cards with negotiable instruments.

Chalmers' Act of 1882 is now exactly a century old . . . and not out. It was undoubtedly a fine piece of legislation.

Dudley Richardson
North Wootton
December 1982

Acknowledgments

The typical examination questions in Part V are reproduced with kind permission of the Law Society and the Institute of Bankers. I am also grateful to Cunard-Brocklebank Ltd for permission to reproduce a bill of lading, to Bass Ltd for permission to reproduce an English share certificate, and to Messrs J Henry Schroder Wagg & Co Ltd for permission to reproduce the American-type share certificate.

Dudley Richardson

Preface to the first edition

Whatever the subject, a book of elementary introduction should endeavour to take the reader from the very beginning to a standard of general attainment. If it attempts to be encyclopaedic as well as introductory it must fail in its object. Consequently, this book is by no means the last word on the law of negotiable instruments and banking. It is hoped, however, that it may be the means of facilitating a study of more advanced works that should follow.

The book has been written with the assumption that the reader has little or no knowledge of elementary law, law of contract, etc. Indeed, the intention of preparing this work was to assist those students of banking who, alas, have made no study of English law. This does not mean that the writer presumes to have supplied a royal road to banking knowledge. He merely hopes that he has made a hard road a little easier (for it is indeed a hard road unless it is preceded by a short study of English law).

The decision to plan the greater part of the book in the form of direct observations, section by section, of the Bills of Exchange Act 1882, is the result of some years of experience in coaching students for the examinations of the Institute of Bankers. It is the writer's firm belief that many of the difficulties encountered by students of this subject arise from a wrong approach, viz., the absorbing of facts, often in tabloid form, divorced from the Act of 1882 from which most of them spring. The codification of the law relating to Bills of Exchange in 1882 was a masterly piece of work. The only way, in the humble opinion of the author, of understanding banking law is a direct study of that work, section by section.

If the writer appears guilty of over-emphasis and repetition here and there, he prays for forgiveness. In a desire to impress certain facts clearly in the mind of the student there may appear a certain measure of over-emphasis to some readers—but it is confined to points of vital importance and to points that in the experience of the author continue with strange regularity to cause the greatest difficulty to the young student of banking.

Dudley Richardson
Nottingham
July 1947

Contents

Part 1
Introductory

Chapter 1
Common law and equity

Common law

Prior to the coming of William the Conqueror, a primitive type of law existed in Harold's Britain based on the customs of the Ancient Britons, Romans and Saxons. The Normans brought with them new customs and legal usages of the Norman French which, being amalgamated with the old customs of Harold's Britain, became the Common Law of England. It concerned chiefly the rights of an individual and his duties towards his fellow citizens. It was, and still is, unwritten, though at times where some old custom has fallen out of use, Parliament has passed an Act re-stating the custom lest it should be forgotten and pass away from common law. Normally, however, Acts of Parliament or statutes are statute law as distinct from our ages-old common law.

In the early days of Norman and Plantagenét kings, common law was our only legal code. It was administered by the King's Courts and in time these courts became known as the Courts of Common Law.

Courts of Common Law

These courts were well known for the jealous and rigid recognition of the ownership of property. If a man was recognised by common law as the legal owner of some property then the courts would afford him all the power of the law to enable him to obtain or retain that property. They would say that he held the legal title to the property. It did not matter how many people had other kinds of interests in it; if one man had the *legal* title and there was no other *legal* interest in the property held by some other person, then the property was his absolutely as far as common law was concerned. Shakespeare leaves evidence of this in his 'Merchant of Venice'. The bond that Antonio gave to Shylock was a right to demand money from Antonio. Shylock was the legal owner of the property represented by the bond. It was a cruel bond but the court never questioned the rights of Shylock to demand its complete fulfilment since Shylock was the *legal* owner of the bond, possessing a *legal* title.

What then do we mean by a 'legal title' or a 'legal interest'? Simply the owning of property (solely or jointly with others) or the owning of an interest or a right in property in such a manner as our old common law has always recognised. This is no peculiar manner of owning property, however. For instance, if I have a gold watch which is undeniably my own property and I transfer it to you for £40 I transfer to you not only the watch but also the legal right to retain it—in other words, I convey to you the legal title. If I have a ship on the high seas and it is legally my property, I can transfer the ship or even a share in the ship to you by completing (or executing) a document of transfer called a deed. In this I should name you as the new owner. In the event of dispute you would produce this deed to the Courts of Common Law and common law would acknowledge you as the legal owner having a legal title to or (where you held only a share) a legal interest in the ship. And of course today, when one acquires any type of property it is the legal title or in other words, the legal estate, that one requires, whether the property be land, jewellery, securities, bills of exchange, etc., since then the common law of England will give one the utmost power to hold and protect the property against all comers.

It follows from all this, of course, that there must be another kind of title to property, another way of having a right to or an interest in property that cannot be called 'legal'. That is so. The one other way of holding property or some interest in it is in the possession of an 'equitable' title or an 'equitable interest'. How this differs from the legal title will be shown later.

Common law has continually been described as rigid and inequitable since it has always been applied without deviation, without consideration of resulting injustice, cruelty, etc. The law is the law, as Antonio discovered with some (temporary) misgivings. Let us take another example. If property had been left by Smith in his will to Brown so that Brown should use the income to maintain Smith's maiden aunt, then the interest in the property that the aunt had was not recognised by common law. And if Brown did not pay the aunt her income that Smith had intended for her she would have received no assistance from the Courts of Common Law. They recognised only Brown, the owner of the legal title conveyed to him by Smith in his will. The only title they acknowledged was the legal title, or the legal estate. But if Smith had left the property to Brown and the aunt jointly then the aunt would have received the help of common law because she would have been a joint *legal* owner and her interest in the property would have been a *legal* interest.

In the case of certain types of property, however, the rigidity of common law expressed itself in another direction. Though it reserved its recognition only for the holder of the legal estate, it refused to recognise on the other hand the right of the legal owner to transfer such property to someone else. Examples of such property were land, choses in action, etc. (see later). It should be noted however that transfers of such property by the legal owner were not *necessarily* illegal. The position was merely that common law refused to acknowledge that any change of ownership had in fact occurred through such a transfer, reserving its recognition to the original owner.

The law of equity
It was not until the reign of Edward III that some serious attempt was made to ameliorate the rigidity and harshness of common law. Though it was never suggested that common law itself should be altered, it was felt that some remedy was required to prevent serious injustices arising from this rigidity. Take the case of the maiden aunt above—if the legal owner of the property (we would call him the trustee today) had refused to pay her the income, she would have had no redress at common law. But such injustices were said to offend the King's conscience since he felt a responsibility for each subject in the kingdom. The Lord Chancellor was the 'Keeper of the King's Conscience' and he eventually acquired power to give judgment and decide cases where under common law there would have been no redress. The maiden aunt could have appealed to the Chancellor, and he in his desire to rectify any situation that offended the King's Conscience or, as we would say today, that was not fair and equitable, would have given orders for the trustee to pay the maiden aunt her income. Since they were the King's orders by virtue of the Chancellor's office, they could not be disobeyed. The Chancellor, however, never overruled common law; he merely supplemented it with a view to ensuring fairness or equity. As his work in this sphere increased it had to be deputed in Edward III's reign to other legal lords in proper courts and these courts came to be known as Courts of Equity. Interests in property such as that held by the maiden aunt were called *equitable interests*

or *interests in equity* (since they were acknowledged only by the Courts of Equity). Later such an interest came to be known as 'an equity' (plural 'equities').

Another right that was recognised only in equity was the right known as 'set-off' or 'counterclaim'. If A owed B £100 for a loan and B owed A £20 for a horse then obviously the whole matter could be settled by A's paying £80 to B. But only the Court of Equity would have acknowledged the right of A to set-off the £20 against the £100. Common law would not have recognised the connection between the two debts. A 'set-off' or 'counterclaim' is consequently an equity.

A third kind of equity that arose was the 'equity of restoration'. Suppose that Jones under threats or under the influence of drink had transferred property to Robinson so that the latter obtained the legal title. Common law would have recognised Robinson as the new legal owner and have ignored Jones completely. But this was inequitable and Jones really had the right to have his property restored—an equitable right or an equity, since only the Court of Equity would assist him. So we find in certain circumstances a person can become the legal owner through, say, fraud, false pretences, threats, etc., but only until such a time as the previous owner takes action through the law of equity to obtain restoration of the property. During that time the title of the new legal owner is subject to the previous owner's equitable right of restoration, i.e., subject to an equity. One can say that his title is, therefore, 'defective' (i.e., imperfect). Most authorities describe it so. A defective title is one subject to this special type of equity. But it should be observed that not every title which is subject to equities can be called defective. It has become customary to speak of the defective title separately from other legal titles affected by equities. Thus, in the study of Negotiable Instruments we commonly use the expression 'subject to defects in title of previous owners and subject to equities'.

We can, then, for the purpose of our study consider equities as fitting one of the following:

(1) An interest of a beneficiary under a trust arising say by a will or settlement.
(2) Set-off or counterclaim.
(3) Right to demand restoration of the legal estate.

Again, though as we observe above, common law would not recognise the right to transfer certain types of property, this right in many cases was recognised by the law of equity. Such transfers were known as equitable transfers (or equitable assignments). If the new owner had difficulty in obtaining or retaining the property and common law refused to recognise him, the Courts of Equity would probably compel the old owner to take legal action on behalf of the new owner to ensure his equitable rights. In other words, an equitable assignee has never had the right under common law to bring a legal action or, as we say, to 'sue in his own name'.

Today, common law still exists separately from equity but the system of maintaining separate courts was finally abolished in 1875. We now have their amalgamation into the High Court. Nevertheless, it is interesting to observe that there are departments known as Divisions of the High Court that still specialise to a great extent in one side or the other. For example, our old Common Law Courts such as the Court of King's Bench have now become the King's (or Queen's) Bench Division, and our Court of Equity or the Chancellor's Court continues in some distinct identity in the Chancery Division.

Chapter 2
Choses in action

What we mean by a chose in action

A man's moveable property can be divided into two types, denoting whether the property is in actual physical possession such as a library of books, a herd of cows, etc., or whether it is property not possessed physically but in the form of a right or an interest in something of value. The former type of property is described as a 'chose in possession' (a 'chose' being a French word meaning a 'thing') and includes all moveable property that is in a material form. If, however, the property does not exist in material shape but is a right—a valuable right that can be enforced in a court of law—then it is a 'chose in action'. Thus, if you have a ton of oranges in your warehouse you have a chose in possession. If you have five pence in coin in your pocket you again have a chose in possession. But if the oranges were in course of shipment, unloaded on a dock or in a shipping company's warehouse, and you held a document showing your *right* to claim the oranges (e.g., a bill of lading, dock warrant, etc.) that *right*, evidenced by the document, would be a chose in action. Again, if you have a postal order for twenty-five pence, you have a *right*, to demand that sum of money from the Post Office; that *right*, evidenced by the postal order, is a chose in action. Further examples of a chose in action are debts, shares in companies, rights under an insurance policy, patents, copyrights, claims to money evidenced by cheques or bills of exchange, etc., etc.

It can be seen from the name itself that it is a 'thing' of value (a chose), immaterial though it may be, that is recognised by law and which can be enforced by 'action' at law, i.e., legal proceedings. The courts if required will uphold your claim and assist you in obtaining all to which you have a right under your chose in action. In nearly every case there will be some document or evidence in writing to prove the right, and the document itself as representative of the right or claim has come to be referred to as the chose in action. It is interesting to note that in the French language, shares in companies are called 'actions'.

The commonest forms of choses in action in commercial use could be grouped under the heading 'Documents of Title' since such documents operate as evidence of the right of some person to money or goods not in that person's actual physical possession.

The document of title is the main proof of ownership and, as it is the means or instrument of obtaining or establishing ownership, it is called an 'instrument'. To obtain music a musician uses an instrument; to undertake an operation a surgeon uses an instrument; to obtain or establish a right to property to which he has a legal right, a man will use an 'instrument'. The word, therefore, is not misused even though it means nothing more substantial than a piece of paper. Thus documents of title are rightly called instruments.

Each instrument refers to a certain property. The person with whom the property is lodged or, more often, the person who is liable to deliver the money, or goods, will be named in the instrument. Similarly, the person who holds the right—the person who can claim the goods or money—will also be mentioned notwithstanding that he may be named or assumed to be merely the bearer of the instrument. The relationship between the two parties is much the same as exists between an ordinary creditor and debtor except that the person who is to pay or deliver (or hold for the time being) the property concerned will have legally bound himself (possibly by his signature) on the instrument. Having legally bound himself, he has, in other words, 'contracted' to fulfil the liability or promise to which the instrument refers. So we say that a document of title also operates as a simple contract between the two people named in the instrument. These two people and their contract are of such fundamental importance to the instrument that they are part of the instrument. And so we call them 'parties' to the instrument.

The chose in action and the law
From the earliest times of English mercantile history it became obvious that if property was not in the owner's physical possession, some evidence of ownership was necessary. Consequently we find that the type of chose in action called documents of title have been in use among traders and merchants for centuries. The English Courts of Common Law in early days gave legal recognition to the document of title and the right of the legal owner of the instrument—a right if necessary to take the case to the courts so as to

obtain his property or to establish his title—in other words, to sue on it in his own name.

But the chose in action was a type of property the *transfer* of which was not recognised by common law. So if Morris had lent Martin £100 and obtained his bond (a document of title) for the loan, the bond was the property of Morris, as far as common law was concerned. If Morris, being short of money later transferred the bond to Richards for £100, then Richards would not have been recognised as the new owner. Of course, this was unimportant if Martin, the debtor, repaid the original loan direct to the new owner at the due time. But if Martin proved awkward, then the new owner, Richards, could not take the case to common law since the Court of Common Law would merely say that the bond was the property of Morris and that he was the man to sue the debtor. So the new owner of the bond could not sue *in his own name;* he was bound to obtain the assistance of the original creditor and plead the case in the latter's name. In short, common law did not recognise the right of an owner of a chose in action to transfer (or assign) his title to the instrument. Unfortunately, if Morris had refused to plead the case at common law on behalf of Richards, then as far as common law was concerned, Richards would lose his £100. But the Courts of Equity recognised a transfer (or assign-ment) of a chose in action, and would compel the transferor (or assignor) to lend his name in any action brought by the transferee (or assignee). But before they would assist a transferee, the latter had to show that notice of the transfer had been given to the per-son about to be sued, i.e., the debtor. So to make a complete transfer, notice of the transfer had to be given to the debtor. This was not unfair since a debtor, normally, has every right to know to whom he owes the money.

There was one 'snag' however. Suppose in the case of Morris and Richards that the original owner of the bond, Morris, owed Martin (the debtor in the bond) twenty pounds for a horse deliv-ered to him before the bond was transferred to Richards. If the bond had never been transferred, then, when Morris had demanded the £100 from Martin, the latter, quite fairly, might have set off the £20 against the £100 and offered Morris £80 in complete settlement. The Court of Common Law, it should be remembered, would not have reconised the right of set-off. They would have insisted on Martin's paying the £100, the question of payment for the horse being the subject for a quite separate action. But the Court of Equity on the other hand would have acknowledged the connection. Martin, by applying to that court could have had the whole matter settled for £80—his right to deduct the £20 as a set-off was not a legal right but an equitable right and was therefore an equity.

The bond of £100, therefore, whilst in the possession of Morris was subject to Martin's equitable right of set-off in the sum of £20. And if Richards, subsequently, as the new owner of the bond had sued Martin in the Court of Equity (the only court that recognised him as the new owner) for £100, Martin still had the right to exercise his right of set-off and offer £80 to Richards as he would have done to Morris. Thus, a new owner, or transferee, of a chose in action was affected by any other private debt of a reverse nature that existed between the original creditor and original debtor before the transfer. The Court of Equity would see justice done in fairness to all. It not only recognised the equitable assignment or transfer of the debt to Richards, but also the equity of £20 in the debt. This meant that to the new owner, the bond was really worth only £80. We therefore say that he took the bond *subject to equities*.

The position can be illustrated in another way by reverting to the case of the maiden aunt of chapter 1. Suppose that the property which the trustee held in trust for the aunt included a chose in action—we have seen that the interest of the aunt was not recognised by common law but only by the Court of Equity. If the trustee transferred the chose in action to a third party, the latter in case of difficulty could obtain his property which the instrument represented only by application to the Court of Equity. Only the latter court recognised the transfer, but at the same time it recognised the interests of the aunt. If the aunt learned that the trustee had betrayed his trust and 'sold' the chose in action, she could apply to the Court of Equity which would force the new owner to pay to the aunt the equivalent of whatever part of the chose in action represented her interest. The new owner could not escape this because the only court that would recognise him as the new owner, recognised also the interest of the aunt. So a transfer or assignment of a chose in action was made subject to the interests in it of third parties—that is, its transfer was subject to equities.

The last illustration. Suppose that A had pledged a chose in action as security to a money-lender for a loan and given the money-lender a written acknowledgement of the latter's interest in it without handing over the actual chose in action. If A subsequently transferred the chose in action to a third party for a sum of money, the new owner's title to the chose in action would have been recognised only by the Court of Equity. But that court also recognised the money-lender's interest in the instrument and when the money-lender discovered that A had dishonestly transferred the chose in action without repaying the loan, the money-lender could apply to the Court of Equity and enforce his rights against the new owner of the instrument. The money-lender's interest was an equitable interest or an equity and the new owner (or the transferee) took the instrument subject to the equity.

The position, therefore, was as follows:

(1) Transfers (or assignments) of a chose in action were recognised only by Courts of Equity and not by common law—it was impossible to make a 'legal' assignment so as to give the new owner a legal title (i.e., a title recognised by common law).

(2) Notice of the assignment had to be given to the person liable on the instrument (i.e., the person who owed the money or held the property for the owner of the instrument).

(3) The assignee (the new owner) of a chose in action could enforce his rights (or sue on the instrument) only in the Court of Equity. This court could compel the original owner to bring an action at common law for the benefit of the assignee but the latter himself could not bring the action—he could not sue in his own name.

(4) The chose in action was transferable subject to equities.

This state of affairs existed until 1873 when the Judicature Act was passed. This statute at long last acknowledged the *legal* assignment of choses in action and consequently common law gave *legal* recognition of the new owner of a chose in action. This meant that a transferee received a *legal* title to a chose in action and if he needed the assistance of the law to obtain the property which the chose in action represented, he could take his case to the Courts of Common Law. His title was, at last, a *legal* title, he became the new legal owner and could sue in the Courts of Common Law in his own name without the assistance of the original owner. This was one step forward. The position had become as follows:

(1) Transfers or assignments of a chose in action were fully recognised at law.

(2) Notice of the assignment had still to be given to the person liable on the instrument.

(3) The assignee could enforce his rights in the Courts of Common Law *and sue in his own name.*

(4) The chose in action remained transferable subject to equities.

The position today with most types of choses in action remains unchanged. A man can make a legal assignment of his life policy (a chose in action) to someone else, but notice of the assignment must be given to the insurance company and the title of the new owner of the policy, though a legal title, is subject to any interest in equity that affected the original owner. For example, the wife of the assured may have some interest in it. Again, there may be a set-off (or counter-claim) held by the insurance company arising from a loan the company has advanced to the original owner. Or if the man in his original proposal to effect the life policy had deliberately misstated facts or had failed to disclose material facts, the company would have the right in equity to demand the restoration to them of the policy—in other words, that original owner's title would be defective.

Chapter 3
The negotiable instrument

Having dealt with the rise and growth of the chose in action we turn to negotiable instruments which are merely a narrow class of choses in action.

It is apparent from the second chapter that the difficulties encountered in dealing with choses in action were:

(1) On each transfer of a chose in action notice had to be given to the party liable.

(2) Each new owner (transferee or assignee) was subject to any equities affecting the title of previous owners (transferors or assignors).

These two features were sufficient to render certain types of choses in action, as we have seen them, clumsy and undesirable for the growing needs of commercial life. It is not surprising, therefore, to find that, in the case of some choses in action in common use among merchants, these two undesirable features were avoided after a time by simply disregarding them. It was mere usage, but the usage came to be recognised by the courts, not under common law or under equity, but under what was known as the Law Merchant (*lex mercatoria*)—a third legal code that maintained its separate identity until the eighteenth century when it was amalgamated with common law—a logical amalgamation since both were based upon customs and usages.

In the case of *Goodwin v Robarts* (1875), the Law Merchant was well defined as 'neither more nor less than the usage of merchants and traders in the different departments of trade, ratified by the decisions of Courts of Law, which, upon such usages being proved before them, have adopted them as settled law.' Long before the Judicature Act of 1873 there had arisen the custom among merchants to transfer by simple delivery (or handing over) certain choses in action so that the transferee obtained a complete *legal* title *without* the requisite notice of the transfer being given to the party liable on the instrument. In addition, provided that the transferee took the instrument in good faith and gave value or some consideration for it to the transferor, he became the full and entire legal owner of the instrument and of all the property it represented, notwithstanding that the previous owner's title was defective or subject to any other equity. Observe the ease of transfer—no memorandum or 'transfer form' giving evidence of the transfer; *no notice to the debtor*—mere delivery by the owner (possibly with his indorsement) was sufficient to transfer a full legal title. And particularly observe that the title passed *free from equities* (provided the transferee gave value and acted in good faith).

These two factors are the decisive features of this narrow class of chose in action and stamp such instruments as *negotiable*. From this we can arrive at the following general definition of a negotiable instrument.

A negotiable instrument is a chose in action, the full and legal title to which is transferable by mere delivery of the instrument (possibly with the transferor's indorsement) with the result that complete ownership of the instrument and all the property it represents passes free from equities to the transferee, providing the latter takes the instrument in good faith and for value.

Observe—(1) A complete transfer is made by mere delivery (or handing over from one person to another), although indorsement by the transferor may be necessary. No notice of the transfer need be given to the party liable.

(2) A full and legal title passes. This means that the transferee can sue in his own name as possessing all rights to the instrument and to the property that the instrument represents.

(3) The title passes free from all equities (including defects in title) to any transferee who, in taking the instrument, gives value for it to the transferor and acts throughout in good faith, i.e., honestly and in complete ignorance of any equity affecting the title of the transferor. (Such a transferee is known as a '*bona fide* transferee for value'. Today he is known as 'a holder in due course'.)

Example   A trustee dishonestly sells to B some bearer bonds and a bill of lading, all belonging to the trust. When this is discovered by the beneficiaries they demand restoration of the property of the trust. They are successful with the bill of lading since it is not a negotiable instrument. The bonds, however, are negotiable. B took them in good faith and for value and consequently he gets a title that is perfect against all the world free from all the equities that attached to the title of the trustee. The only remedy for the beneficiaries is to sue the latter—for what it is worth. Note that in each case here, the trustee had a legal title.

Let us suppose in addition then, that the trustee stole a bearer bill of exchange from his employer and sold that too to B. This document is a negotiable instrument and B, by taking it in good faith and giving value gets a perfect full legal title. Although the transferor is a thief *with no title at all*, yet the transferee, B, gets a perfect title.

The general rule of law is that when a man purchases property from another, his title to the property will be no better than that held by the person who sold the goods to him. If the man innocently buys from a thief then he will have no right to retain the goods since the thief has no right to them. If he buys from a person whose title is subject to equities then his title is no better and is subject to the same equities. But with the negotiable instrument we can see we are outside the general rule of law. Here, a *bona fide* transferee for value can get a perfect title free from equities even though the transferor's title is subject to equities–or further, even if the transferor was say a thief with no title at all.

Today, bills of exchange (which of course include cheques), promissory notes (which of course include bank notes), dividend warrants, interest warrants, bearer bonds, bearer scrip, debentures payable to bearer, share warrants payable to bearer, Treasury Bills, certificates of deposit issued by commercial banks; all these are negotiable instruments providing they are in a deliverable state, i.e., in favour of 'the bearer'. Most of these are such in origin. Bills of exchange, cheques, dividend warrants and interest warrants are often drawn in favour of a specified person, however, and will need the indorsement of such a person to create the deliverable state. On the other hand, some documents of title to *money* or security for *money* such as postal orders, money orders, share certificates, insurance policies and debentures, and documents of title to *goods*, such as bills of lading, are not negotiable. The only way of finding if a certain document of value is negotiable is to see whether all the three features of negotiability (see p. 15) are found in the instrument itself or in its use. If any one is missing then the document is not negotiable. For example, a share certificate, an example of which is given on the opposite page, is not negotiable because feature number one is not apparent. A share certificate is not transferable by mere delivery or indorsement and delivery. A form of transfer is needed to evidence the change of ownership, and notification of the transfer has to be given to the company concerned (i.e., the party liable) by sending the transfer for registration.

Again, although a bill of lading (a document of title to goods) is freely transferable by delivery (with indorsement) like negotiable instruments, it is nevertheless not negotiable. This is because

SPECIMEN SHARE CERTIFICATE

No.

51800

Ordinary Shares
of 5/- each

BASS, MITCHELLS & BUTLERS LIMITED

Incorporated under the Companies Act, 1948

This is to Certify *that* SPECIMEN.

Proprietor(s) of ....is/are registered as the ....fully-paid

Ordinary Shares of 5s. each in BASS, MITCHELLS & BUTLERS LIMITED, subject to the

Memorandum and Articles of Association thereof.

Given *under the Common Seal of the Company*

the .... *day of* ...., 19 ....

The Company will not transfer any Shares without the production of a Certificate relating to such Shares, which Certificate must be surrendered before any Transfer
whether for the whole or any portion thereof can be registered or a new Certificate issued in exchange.

TRANSFER OFFICE:—National Provincial Registrars Limited, P.O. Box No. 71, 22, Old Broad Street, London, E.C.2

mercantile usage has decided that the title to goods cannot in normal circumstances pass free trom any equities that affected the title of a previous owner, and a person who buys a bill of lading from a thief will be compelled to restore the bill of lading to the true owner and all the goods it represents.

So far, we have used the words 'assign' and 'transfer' as though they were synonymous. This is not quite true. Though they both represent a change of ownership of an instrument of value there is a difference in the method used in each case. When referring to documents of title we should use the word 'transferable' only when we mean that the document is freely transferable by delivery (or indorsement and delivery), like the negotiable instrument, without notice being given to the party liable. In this way, a bill of lading is transferable. The word 'assignable', however, implies a change of ownership by the completion of a separate document evidencing the transfer and giving notice to the party liable. Thus, a share certificate is not, strictly speaking, transferable but assignable, since the title to the shares does not pass to the new owner by mere delivery of the certificate but by the completion of a separate transfer form which is registered at the company's office. This registration acts as notice to the party liable—the company is the party liable since it has accepted money for the shares and is responsible to the shareholder. Other examples of assignable documents are life policies, certificates of government stock, debentures, etc.

Why is it that in the development of commerce some instruments have come to be recognised as negotiable and possessing the three main characteristics given above, whilst others have remained either only transferable or only assignable? In almost every case the answer can be found in mercantile usage. The goldsmith's receipt for money lodged with him (the forebear of the present bank note) came to be transferred freely by mere delivery although at first, doubtlessly, notice of the transfer was given to the goldsmith. These receipts became the 'currency' of commerce and to have insisted on notice of transfer each time would have put a brake on commerce. Thus it became customary to dispense with notice, and at the same time it became customary to treat the goldsmith's receipt as entirely free from the interests of third parties, etc. (i.e., free from equities) otherwise their utility would have been drastically curtailed. In like manner, other instruments took upon themselves all the features of negotiability. In the event of any legal dispute, the court's decisions have been guided by mercantile customs and the courts have upheld such customs. The

Law Merchant was not a code of mercantile laws laid down in the very beginnings of commerce but a legal recognition of the usages of trade that had already become permanent features of English commercial life.

In some very isolated cases, statute law (Acts of Parliament) has pronounced a certain instrument negotiable, though generally after established usage (e.g., the negotiability of a bill of exchange had been generally recognised long before 1882, but in that year the Bills of Exchange Act gave statutory recognition to that negotiability).

In the past, many cases of dispute over instruments of title have been brought before the courts. It can be imagined that if the ownership of a certain instrument was under contention, then the court's decision might easily have depended on whether the instrument was negotiable or not. If the holder of the instrument could prove it was negotiable then he could defeat, for example, anyone claiming to have an equitable interest in it. The courts have had the task of deciding from time to time whether a variety of individual documents were in the negotiable class or not, and from their decisions it has been possible to get the negotiable instrument more sharply defined and the position generally clarified. From these decisions, three requirements have appeared.

(1) No instrument can be called negotiable even though it belongs to a class of instruments considered negotiable if it bears evidence on its face to destroy or negative its negotiability (e.g., although cheques are recognised as negotiable, a cheque that has been marked 'not negotiable' obviously cannot be a negotiable instrument). Though its negotiability is lost, we must bear in mind that it is still freely transferable though subject to defects in title of any prior parties. 'Negotiability' is *not* a synonym of transferability.

(2) It is not sufficient that a certain individual instrument be accepted with all the characteristics of negotiability by the parties concerned—it must belong to a class of instruments considered negotiable in mercantile usage. Attempts have at times been made to get certain documents of title to *goods* acknowledged as negotiable, but they have failed. Why? Because mercantile usage has considered negotiable only those documents that constitute a promise or obligation to pay *money* or deliver securities for *money*.

(3) Mercantile usage is essential. There must exist a mercantile custom to treat the instrument, or the class of instrument to

which it belongs, as negotiable. Although the custom can be traced over two or three centuries in most cases, an old origin is not absolutely essential, nor is the usage bound to be an English one.

Having found what instruments are negotiable and what rights can accrue to anyone becoming the owner of such an instrument, we must bear in mind that these rights do not automatically obtain unless certain requirements are fulfilled. We have already observed two requirements, viz.:

(1) The transfer must be for value (i.e., the transferee must give something of value or render some service in exchange for the instrument, and not merely take it as a gift).

(2) The transferee must be *bona fide*, i.e., act in good faith.

Besides these, the instrument itself must be:

(3) Complete and regular on the face of it.

(4) In a deliverable state.

If these four requirements are not fulfilled, the transferee may find that some or all of the powers usually accruing to the holder of a negotiable instrument are lost, and his title to the instrument incomplete, affected by equities or entirely non-existing. These four requirements deserve further investigation.

The transfer must be for value

This is self-explanatory. The transferee must give some value, goods, money or services generally, to the transferor as the consideration for the transfer. But observe that the value or consideration could quite effectively be a promise to deliver the value as and when the transferee required it (e.g., a man deposits bearer bonds at a bank as security for a loan. The bank obtains a complete legal title to the bonds immediately although the value required has not yet passed, the agreement to the loan being considered sufficient consideration). Again, particularly concerning bank notes, cheques and bills of exchange, the value will be acknowledged although it may have been given in the past: (e.g., I order a ton of coal but delay payment until the month-end when I send a cheque. Although the coal was delivered some time before and not in anticipation of the actual individual cheque, the merchant, in accepting the cheque as payment for the coal, has undoubtedly given value for it). The same provision is found in section 27 of the Bills of Exchange Act 1882, which states 'valuable consideration may be constituted by . . . any antecedent debt or liability'.

But it does not follow that no title can be obtained to a negotiable instrument if value has not been given, when, for example, the instrument is transferred as a gift. The instrument would still be negotiable but the transferee might not have the advantages of all the features of a negotiable instrument. His title would be complete and perfect only if the person from whom he received the instrument had a complete and perfect title. But if the transferor's title was subject to equities then the negotiable instrument, transferred as a gift, would not pass free from those equities.

A widely held but mistaken idea is that the value given must be adequate. This is not so. If you hand me your gold watch and I give you a penny for it, I give value for the watch, no matter how inadequate the value may appear. There is one proviso; the value must be apparent and not illusory. Let us take an example. Bank of England notes, being promissory notes, are fully negotiable. So a person who takes them in good faith and for value gets a full and complete title to them, free from equities, in spite of the fact that the transferor has stolen them. Now if a very shifty-eyed vagabond offered me a £50 Bank of England note for five pence and I was foolish enough to accept the offer, my title to the note would be very difficult to establish, obviously. But why? Because I had not given value? No! The law does *not* require *adequate* value and would recognise the five pence that I gave, as value. Why then would it be difficult for me to establish my title? Because I should find it almost impossible to prove I had acted in *good faith*, since the very circumstances should have made me suspect the note to be stolen property. Thus we turn to good faith.

Good faith
No hard and fast rule can be laid down on this aspect. Whether a man acts in good faith or not is entirely a question of the facts of the individual case. Should dispute over the ownership of a negotiable instrument come to the courts, then the case will be judged on its merits or demerits as far as the good faith of the party or parties involved is concerned. However, from past legal decisions the following overriding principle emerges.

To prove his good faith, a transferee of a negotiable instrument must be able to show that he acted honestly and had no knowledge of any defect in the title of the transferor of the instrument or any suspicion thereof. This does *not* mean that a man acts in bad faith merely because you or I or any normally intelligent person, in similar circumstances, would have 'smelt a rat' and have doubted whether the transferor was in fact the true owner of the instrument. A man may act carelessly or display little intelligence in not becoming aware of the transferor's defective title or not even becoming a little suspicious; nevertheless, if it is shown that he did *not* become aware of the defect, that his suspicions were *not* aroused and that he did *not* deliberately blind himself to any suspicious fact, then his good faith will not be held in doubt. To put it briefly, we can say that the question of negligence does not concern good faith. Incidentally, section 90 of the Bills of Exchange Act 1882, repeats the same point:

> A thing is deemed to be done in good faith within the meaning of this Act where it is in fact done honestly, whether it is done negligently or not.

Complete and regular on the face of it

No instrument is negotiable in the full sense of the word unless it appears complete in every essential feature. For instance, a cheque is capable of being a negotiable instrument, but a cheque without the name of the payee, or one with no amount filled in is not negotiable, but is what the Bills of Exchange Act 1882, calls an inchoate (incomplete) instrument. Suppose a cheque is drawn by Smith leaving the name of the payee blank and Smith sends the cheque to Jones who subsequently transfers it to Brown. Brown may give value for the cheque and act in complete good faith, but he cannot be certain of a perfect title (as he could had the cheque been fully negotiable). Should the title of Jones be subject to equities, Brown will be similarly affected. The transferee may be authorised to complete it, but even if he does complete it within the scope of the authority, the instrument cannot be recognised as negotiable *whilst in his hands* because he did not *receive* it complete and regular on the face of it. The subject of inchoate instruments is examined further under section 20 of the Bills of Exchange Act 1882.

Deliverable state

In our study of the growth of the negotiable instrument, we found that one of its essential characteristics was its ease of transfer, viz., by delivery or indorsement and delivery. We found that the transferor merely handed the instrument to the transferee (of course, it could be delivered just as effectively by post or any other agent). But we observed that delivery may have to be completed by the transferor's indorsement. When, then, is mere delivery sufficient and when must that indorsement accompany it?

A negotiable instrument must indicate the person(s) to whom it is payable or in whose favour it is written (i.e., to whom the property in the instrument belongs). Some negotiable instruments will state that the money belongs to the *bearer* of the instrument; there will be instructions in the instrument, addressed to the party who has to pay, instructing him to hand the money (or security for money) to the *bearer* of the document. In this case, the instrument is said to be drawn in favour of (and therefore payable to) the bearer. This is true even if the instructions to pay or deliver indicate a certain person by name with the additional words 'or bearer'. For example, a cheque payable to 'John Smith or bearer' is as much a 'bearer' instrument as one payable merely to 'bearer'. Any negotiable instrument that is at the outset payable to bearer will always be in a deliverable state. Smith, in the example, could transfer the instrument to Brown by merely handing it to him (as he would with a pound note for example).

But the wording of the instrument may order payment to a certain person, e.g., a cheque payable to 'John Smith' or one payable to 'John Smith or order'. Smith, in this case, can transfer the cheque to his friend Brown so that it will then be payable to Brown, but to make delivery complete, he must indorse the cheque 'John Smith'. The indorsement of John Smith which facilitates the transfer can be in the form of either:

(a) the mere signature of John Smith, or

(b) his signature, together with the words 'pay William Brown'.

The simple indorsement of (a) is called an indorsement in blank whereas that in (b) is known as a special indorsement. More will be said later of these indorsements in section 2 of the Bills of Exchange Act 1882. Meanwhile we should note that in both cases the indorsement *puts the instrument in a deliverable state*, with the effect that in (a) it is in a deliverable state for transfer to anyone and in (b) in a deliverable state for transfer *only to William Brown*. Therefore at this early stage of our study it should already be clear that an indorsement in blank of an instrument not payable to bearer does in fact convert such an instrument into just such a bearer instrument.

One can see then in the above case that the indorsement in one form or the other is essential, and should it be missing, then

Brown's position will not be as secure as it would be normally with a negotiable instrument. If the title of Smith is subject to equities then Brown's title also will be subject to the same equities. Even if there are no equities, Brown's title is still unsatisfactory, since if he has to take action in court to enforce payment, he cannot do so in his own name (i.e., he cannot sue in his own name). He would require Smith to initiate proceedings for him in Smith's name. In fact, he would have no legal title at all, but merely an equitable one. But with it would be the right to demand the indorsement of Smith. The *legal* title passes only when delivery is made, and here, delivery without the indorsement is not a delivery recognised by common law or the Law Merchant. Further, the right to demand the indorsement is, with most negotiable instruments only an equitable right, although with regard to bills of exchange (including cheques) the right to obtain this indorsement is now a legal one by virtue of section 31 (4) of the Bills of Exchange Act 1882.

It should be observed, however, that the indorsement need not necessarily be made at the time of delivery; it can be done before or after delivery. For example, if I have a cheque for £10 payable to me and you give me £10 for it only to find when I have gone that I have omitted to indorse it, you can at any time later secure my indorsement and delivery will be complete. But supposing that before you found me again to obtain the indorsement, you learned that my title to the cheque was defective since I had obtained the cheque by fraud, then your title would be defective as mine had been, since you could not be a *bona fide* transferee (i.e., you would have become aware of the defect or equity prior to the completion of the transfer).

The word 'negotiable'
On p. 18 the difference between the words 'transfer' and 'assign' was explained and we saw that a transferable instrument (not necessarily a negotiable instrument) is one that can pass from one owner to another merely by delivery or indorsement and delivery. Such is the case with a bill of lading which is transferable, but, because it cannot be transferred free from existing equities, is not negotiable.

A negotiable instrument is consequently in a narrow class of transferable instruments, since in addition to being transferable by delivery, it also passes free from existing equities to a *bona fide* transferee for value. Frequently, however, it will be found that some writers use the word 'negotiate' when they mean 'transfer for value by delivery'. Thus they may say that a certain instrument was *negotiated* by Smith to Brown in spite of the fact that such an instrument is not negotiable—obviously they mean 'transferred by delivery for value'. A good example of this will be met later in this book on the subject of 'Conditional orders'. (See p. 188). The Cheques Act 1957, includes the sentence, 'The foregoing provisions of this Act do not make negotiable any instrument which, apart from them, is not negotiable'—and here it may well be that the person who drafted the Act meant *'transferable'* and not 'negotiable'.

It is common, therefore, to see the word 'negotiable' loosely used merely to denote 'transferable by delivery', but always remember that the essence of the word 'negotiable' is the *power to transfer free from equities*.

Negotiability by estoppel

On p. 19 it will be observed that an instrument cannot be recognised as negotiable unless it belongs to a certain class of negotiable instrument. That remains correct. But it is possible for a non-negotiable instrument to be treated temporarily as negotiable in a certain transaction and for the benefit of certain parties. An example will make this clear.

Brown is the owner of certain bonds worth £1,000 that are assignable instruments but not recognised as negotiable. He borrows £500 from a moneylender and delivers the bonds as security, leading the moneylender to believe that the bonds are negotiable; (his reason for misleading the moneylender was no doubt because negotiable bonds are first-class security whereas non-negotiable bonds without deeds of transfer might not have been acceptable security to the moneylender). Some time later, the moneylender obtains an overdraft from his bank for £1,000 and deposits Brown's bonds as security. When Brown eventually comes to repay the moneylender and demands return of his bonds he finds that the moneylender has disappeared. He turns to the bank and points out that when the bonds were transferred to the moneylender, he had an equity in the bonds to the extent of £500, i.e., the moneylender's interest in the bonds was only to the extent of the loan of £500, the remaining £500 being Brown's own interest which the moneylender had no authority to transfer to the bank. He

SPECIMEN BILL OF LADING

Shipper		BILL OF LADING	UK Customs Assigned No.	B/L No.

Shipper's Ref.

F / Agent's Ref.

ACL

an affiliate of:
Compagnie Générale Maritime
Cunard Steam-Ship Company Ltd.
Intercontinental Transport (I.C.T.) B.V.
Swedish American Line
Swedish Transatlantic Line
Wallenius Line

Consignee (If 'Order' state Notify Party and Address)

Notify Party and Address (leave blank if stated above)

Pre-Carriage By*	Place of Receipt by Pre-Carrier*
Vessel	Port of Loading
Port of Discharge	Place of Delivery by On-Carrier*

Marks and Nos; Container No.	Number and kind of packages, description of goods	Gross Weight	Measurement

Freight details, charges, etc

RECEIVED by ACL for shipment by ocean vessel, between port of loading and port of discharge, and for arrangement or procurement of pre-carriage from place of receipt and on-carriage to place of delivery where stated above, the goods as specified above in apparent good order and condition unless otherwise stated. The goods to be delivered at the above mentioned port of discharge or place of delivery, whichever applicable. Subject always to the exceptions, limitations, conditions and liberties set out on the reverse side hereof, to which the merchant agrees by accepting this B/L. In WITNESS whereof TWO (2) original Bs/L have been signed, if not otherwise stated below, one of which being accomplished the other (s) to be void.

Ocean Freight Payable at	Place and date of Issue
Number of Original Bs/L	Signature

For ACL
CUNARD-BROCKLEBANK LIMITED, AS AGENTS ONLY

*Applicable only when document used as a Through B/L.

Printed in England by Rockliff Brothers Ltd., 2 Rumford Street, Liverpool 2

Atlantic Container Line Groupment D'Interet Economique Regi Par L'Ordonnance du 23 September 1967
Atlantic Container Line Services Ltd., Atlantic House, Herbert Walker Avenue, Western Docks, Southampton SO9 1HA, England.
Atlantic Container Line Ltd., 80 Pine Street, New York, N.Y. 10005

GENERAL AGENTS: (United Kingdom Trade)

Liverpool	Cunard-Brocklebank Limited, ACL Division, Cunard House, Cotton Exchange Building, Old Hall Street, Liverpool L3 9BN
Southampton	Cunard-Brocklebank Limited, South Western House, Canute Road, Southampton SO9 1ZA
Glasgow	Anchor Line Ltd., 59 Waterloo Street, Glasgow G2 7BU

OFFICES:

Birmingham	Cunard-Brocklebank Limited, 148 Edmund Street, Birmingham B3 2JP
Bradford	Cunard-Brocklebank Limited, Midland House, Cheapside, Bradford BD1 4LW
Bristol	Cunard-Brocklebank Limited, Friary House, 15 Colston Street, Bristol BS1 5AP
London	Cunard-Brocklebank Limited, Chobham Farm, Leyton Road, Stratford, London E15 1DG
Baltimore	Ramsay Scarlett & Co., Inc., 19/21 South Street, Baltimore, Md. 21202
Hampton Roads, Norfolk Portsmouth	Ramsay Scarlett & Co., Inc., First & Merchants Building. Suite 200, 300 East Main Street, Norfolk VA 23510
Montreal	Atlantic Container Line (Canada) Ltd., 465 St. John St., Montreal 125 PQ
Toronto	Atlantic Container Line (Canada) Ltd., 159 Bay Street, Toronto
Halifax	Atlantic Container Line (Canada) Ltd., P.O. Box 3188 Halifax South Postal Station, Halifax, Nova Scotia B3J 3H5

Endorsements

1. DEFINITIONS. Where ACL is mentioned in this Bill of Lading it means "Atlantic Container Line Groupment D'Interet Economique Regi Par L'Ordonnance du 23 September 1967". Merchant means and includes the Shipper, the Consignee, the Holder of this Bill of Lading, the Receiver and the Owner of the goods.

2. CONTRACTING PARTIES. The contract evidenced by this B/L is between the Merchant and ACL and it is agreed that ACL only shall be liable as Carrier under this contract.

3. RESPONSIBILITY.
I. ACL shall be responsible for the goods from the time when the goods are received by ACL at the sea terminal at the port of loading to the time when they are delivered or despatched by ACL from the sea terminal at the port of discharge and also during any previous or subsequent period of carriage by water under this Bill of Lading subject to the Hague Rules contained in the International Convention for the unification of certain rules relating to Bills of Lading dated 25th August, 1924, and any legislation making those rules compulsorily applicable to this Bill of Lading, including the Carriage of Goods by Sea Act of the United States of America, approved 16th April, 1936, or the Canadian Water Carriage of Goods Act, 1936. It is agreed, that such rules and legislation shall also apply to deck cargo and shall be deemed to incorporate (where this is not already the case) the amendments to the Hague Rules contained in the Protocol signed at Brussels on 23rd February 1968 (The Hague-Visby Rules).

II. When either the place of receipt or place of delivery set forth herein is an inland point in the USA, Canada or Europe, the responsibility of ACL with respect to the transportation to and from the sea terminal ports will be as follows:
(a) Between points in Europe, to transport the goods.
(1) if by road, in accordance with the Convention on the Contract for the International Carriage of Goods by Road, dated 19th May, 1956 (CMR);
(2) if by rail, in accordance with the International Agreement on Railway Transports, dated 25th February, 1961 (CIM);
(3) if by air, in accordance with the Convention for the Unification on certain Rules relating to International Carriage by Air, signed Warsaw 12th October, 1929, as amended by the Hague Protocol, dated 28th September, 1955.
(b) Between points in the USA or Canada, to procure transportation by carriers (one or more) authorized by competent authority to engage in transportation between such points, and such transportation shall be subject to the inland carrier's contracts of carriage and tariffs. ACL guarantees the fulfilment of such inland carrier's obligations under their Contracts and tariffs.

III. As to services incident to through transportation, ACL undertakes to procure such services as necessary. All such services will be subject to the usual contracts of persons providing the services. ACL guarantees the fulfilment of the obligations of such persons under the pertinent contracts.

IV. When the goods have been damaged or lost during through-transportation and it can not be established in whose custody the goods were when the damage or loss occurred, the damage or loss shall be deemed to have occurred during the sea voyage and the Hague Rules as defined above shall apply.

V. ACL does not accept responsibility for any direct or indirect loss or damage sustained by the Merchant through delay, unless ACL is liable for consequences of delay under any laws, statutes, agreements or conventions of a mandatory nature.

VI. No servant or agent of ACL or any independent contractor or subcarrier employed by ACL to carry out any of its obligations hereunder shall, in any circumstances whatsoever, be under any greater liability to the Merchant than ACL for any loss, damage or delay howsoever caused to the goods, but shall be entitled to the benefit of every exemption, limitation, condition and liberty herein contained in favour of ACL. For the purpose of this provision all such persons shall be deemed to be parties to the contract evidenced by this Bill of Lading made on their behalf by ACL.

4. PACKING AND MERCHANT-OWNED EQUIPMENT. The Merchant shall be liable for any loss, damage or injury caused by faulty packing of goods within containers and trailers and on flats when such packing has been performed by the Merchant or on behalf of the Merchant.
ACL does not accept responsibility for the functioning of reefer containers or trailers, not owned nor leased by ACL.

5. ROUTE. The goods may be carried by any route whatsoever, whether or not the most direct or advertised or customary route, via any ports or places in any order whatsoever and for whatsoever purpose visited, together with other goods of every kind, dangerous or otherwise whether stowed on or under deck. Vessels may sail with or without pilots, undergo repairs, adjust equipment, drydock and tow vessels in all situations.

6. SUBSTITUTION OF VESSEL AND TRANSHIPMENT. ACL has the right, but not the obligation, to carry the goods by any substitute vessel, or by any other means of transport whether by water, land or air, and may discharge the goods at any place for transhipment, tranship, land or store the goods either on shore or afloat and reship or forward the same.

7. DECK SHIPMENT. ACL shall be entitled to carry the goods on deck in containers.

8. DELIVERY OF GOODS. If the goods are not taken by the Merchant within a reasonable time of ACL calling upon him to take delivery ACL shall be at liberty to put the goods in safe custody on behalf of the Merchant at the Merchant's risk and expense.

9. FREIGHT AND CHARGES

a) Freight to be paid in cash without discount and whether prepayable or payable at destination, to be considered as earned on receipt of the goods and not to be returned, goods lost or not lost.

b) Freight and all other amounts mentioned in this B/L are, at the option of ACL, to be paid in the currency named in this B/L or of the country of the port of loading or port of discharge, at the highest selling rate of exchange for banker's sight draft current on the date of the freight agreement or on the date of this B/L, or for prepayable freight on the day of loading, or for freight payable at destination on the day, when the vessel is entered at the Customs House or on the date of withdrawal of the delivery order. If ACL has consented to payment of freight and charges in other currencies than U.S. or Canadian Dollars and such other currencies are devalued before payment, then the conversion of U.S. or Canadian currencies shall be effected at the highest bank selling rate on the date of payment.

c) All dues, taxes and charges or other expenses in connection with the goods shall be paid by the Merchant.

d) The Marchant shall reimburse ACL in proportion to the amount of freight for any increase of war risk insurance premium and war risk increase of the wages of the Master, officers and crew and for any increase of the cost for bunkers and for deviation or delay caused by war or warlike operations or by government directions in such connection.

e) The Merchant warrants the correctness of the declaration of contents, insurance, weight, measurement or value of the goods but ACL reserves the right to have the contents inspected in order to ascertain the weight, measurement or value for the purpose of verifying the freight basis. If on such inspection it is found that the declaration is not correct it is agreed that a sum equal either to five times the difference between the correct freight and the freight charged or to double the correct freight less the freight charged, whichever sum is the smaller shall be payable as liquidated damages to ACL notwithstanding any other sum having been stated on the B/L as freight payable.

10. LIEN. ACL shall have a lien on the cargo for any amount due under this contract and for cost of recovering same and shall be entitled to sell the goods privately or by auction without prior notice, advertisement or legal authority to cover any claim. If on sale of the goods, the proceeds fail to cover the amount due and the cost and expense incurred, ACL shall be entitled to recover the difference from the Merchant.

11. GENERAL AVERAGE. General Average to be adjusted at any port or place at ACL's option, and to be settled according to the York-Antwerp Rules 1974. In the event of accident, danger, damage or disaster before or after commencement of the voyage resulting from any cause whatsoever, whether due to negligence or not, for which or for the consequence of which ACL is not responsible by statute, contract or otherwise, the Merchant shall contribute with ACL in General Average to the payment of any sacrifice, losses of expenses of a General Average nature that may be made or incurred, and shall pay salvage and special charges incurred in respect of the goods. If a salving vessel is owned or operated by ACL, salvage shall be paid for as fully as if the salving vessel or vessels belonged to strangers. Such deposit, as ACL or its agents without prejudice may deem sufficient to cover the estimated contribution of the goods and any salvage and special charges thereon, shall, if required, be paid to ACL or its agents prior to delivery into a special account in accordance with the provisions of the said Rules.

12. OPTIONS OF ACL. If it shall be considered by ACL at any time that the performance or continued performance of this contract may subject the ocean vessel, her crew and cargo or other transport to any hindrance, risk, delay, difficulty or disadvantage of whatsoever kind, ACL shall be entitled; whether or not the events in question existed or were anticipated at the time of entering into this contract, if the carriage has not already commenced, to cancel this contract, or, in any event, to discharge, tranship, land or deliver the goods at any convenient port or place or to forward them at the sole risk and expense of the Merchant, or otherwise to deal with the goods as ACL may think advisable under the particular circumstances. In any such event ACL shall be entitled to full freight and to a reasonable extra compensation for any service rendered to the goods.

13. JURISDICTION. Disputes arising under this Bill of Lading shall be determined at the option of the Merchant either by the Commercial Court in London in accordance with English law or by the U.S. District Court for the Southern District of New York in accordance with the laws of the United States. For traffic to or from Canada jurisdiction will be limited to the Commercial Court in London only.

GOODS OF DANGEROUS OR DAMAGING NATURE AND RADIOACTIVE MATERIAL MUST NOT BE TENDERED FOR SHIPMENT UNLESS WRITTEN NOTICE OF THEIR NATURE AND THE NAME AND ADDRESS OF THE SENDER AND THE RECEIVER HAVE BEEN PREVIOUSLY GIVEN TO ACL. SUB-CARRIERS, MASTER OR AGENT OF THE VESSEL AND THE NATURE IS DISTINCTLY MARKED ON THE OUTSIDE OF THE PACKAGE OR PACKAGES AS REQUIRED BY APPLICABLE STATUTES OR REGULATIONS AND IN ADDITION ON EACH CONTAINER, FLAT, TRAILER ETC. A SPECIAL STOWAGE ORDER GIVING CONSENT TO SHIPMENT MUST ALSO BE OBTAINED FROM ACL. THE MERCHANT WILL BE LIABLE FOR ALL CONSEQUENTIAL DAMAGE AND EXPENSE IF ALL THE FOREGOING PROVISIONS ARE NOT COMPLIED WITH.

Rev. 4/78

claims his 'share' of £500 from the bank on the grounds that as the bonds are not negotiable, the title of the bank to the bonds is subject to equities, in this case subject to his equity of £500. According to the strict general interpretation of the law, his claim appears to be sound. But it does not seem right that Brown should wrongly lead the moneylender to believe the bonds negotiable to obtain a loan that he could not otherwise have obtained and then later deny negotiability when it suits him—to put it bluntly, he cannot have it both ways. The court will say that by his previous actions, he will not be allowed to plead that the bonds are not negotiable, i.e., he will be 'estopped from denying their negotiability'. For the purposes of the two transactions involved the bonds will be treated as negotiable, and consequently, the bank will be able to retain the bonds free from the equity of Brown. This does not mean that the bonds from thenceforward will be considered negotiable. The bank's title will be upheld, but thereafterwards the bonds must be regarded as non-negotiable.

The term 'negotiable by estoppel', is not considered to be a good description, however, since the bonds do not become generally negotiable but merely acquire the qualities of negotiability during a certain transaction.

Rights of a holder to sue on a negotiable instrument

A *bona fide* holder for value (in the Bills of Exchange Act he is called a 'holder in due course') can, if necessary, sue every person who signed the instrument prior to him. This is known as a *right of recourse* and arises if the party primarily liable on the instrument fails to meet his obligation. The more parties there are to such an instrument the more likelihood there will be for the owner of the instrument to obtain what is due to him.

Exceptions:
(1) Infants and enemy nationals during wartime, etc., cannot be sued since they are incapable of being the subject of a legal action.
(2) A dividend may be claimed from a Trustee in bankruptcy but a bankrupt cannot be sued personally.
(3) A party can avoid the liability on the instrument to future holders by adding the words *'sans recours'* or 'without recourse to me' to his signature.
(4) A person whose signature has been forged cannot be sued since he has not signed the instrument. But if he leads others

to accept the forgery as his genuine signature then he may be liable as though he had actually signed: in legal terms he will be 'estopped from denying the forgery'.

Quasi-negotiable instruments

There are certain choses in action which, though not fully negotiable, possess some of the characteristics of a negotiable instrument and are called quasi-negotiable. Under this heading are found Bills of Lading, American Share Certificates and IOU's.

Bills of lading

A bill of lading (see pp. 26–27 for specimen bill) is a document of title to goods and is used extensively in foreign trade. It operates also as evidence of a contract for the carriage of goods from one port to another and is issued by the master of a ship. Its main importance however lies in its value as a document of title.

> **Example** A London merchant arranges to buy 1,000 crates of oranges from a Spanish exporter. The Spaniard arranges with a shipping company to carry the oranges to London on a certain ship. The master of the ship sailing to London will take the oranges on board and issue a receipt for them. This receipt is intended to be the means of claiming the oranges on arrival in London. It also operates as evidence of an agreement to carry the consignment to London—in short it is a bill of lading. The bill of lading is sent by air mail to the Londoner's bank or some other agent for passage to the importer if satisfactory arrangements have been made as to payment. The Londoner awaits the arrival of the ship and then claims the oranges by presenting the bill of lading which is exchanged for the consignment. But if the Londoner sells the oranges before the ship arrives then all he need do is to indorse the bill of lading and transfer it to the buyer. The latter will then be able to claim the oranges when the ship berths, as before.

We have already observed that because a bill of lading is not a contract to pay money or security for money it cannot be considered negotiable. Therefore, though it passes freely from a transferor to a transferee by delivery it does not pass free from equities, if any exist. If it is obtained by false pretences and subsequently transferred by the fraudulent person to a *bona fide* transferee for value, the latter cannot take a full legal title to the goods since his title is subject to an equity, viz., the right of the true owner of the instrument to the restoration of his property. A further example.

AMERICAN SHARE CERTIFICATE

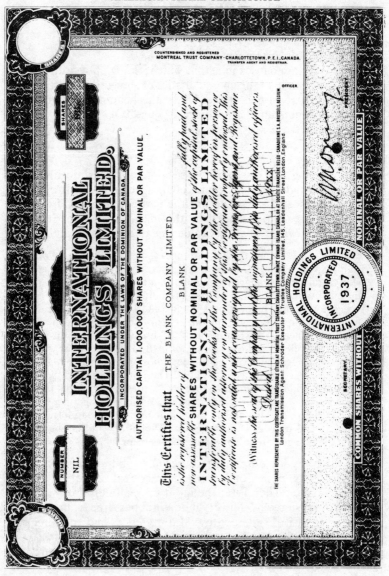

For value Received _____ *hereby sell assign and transfer unto*

_____ *Shares*

of the Capital Stock represented by the within Certificate and do hereby irrevocably

constitute and appoint _____ *Attorney*

to transfer the said stock in the Books of the within named Company with full power

of substitution in the premises.

Dated _____

In presence of _____

NOTICE: THE SIGNATURE TO THIS ASSIGNMENT MUST CORRESPOND
WITH THE NAME AS WRITTEN ON THE FACE OF THE CERTIFICATE,
IN EVERY PARTICULAR, WITHOUT ALTERATION OR ENLARGEMENT,
OR ANY CHANGE WHATEVER.

If B is the holder of a bill of lading in which A has a financial interest, then, although B can legally transfer the instrument, the equity held by A will remain attached, and the person who eventually claims the goods will have to satisfy the claims of A. The equity however does not render the bill non-transferable.

One further point of interest. A consignor of goods has the right to stop goods in transit if he hears that the consignee has become insolvent, notwithstanding that the consignee has received the bill of lading from the consignor. But if the consignee has transferred the bill of lading to a third party, then the right to stop transit is lost.

Bills of exchange are a separate study in themselves and outside the scope of this book. Our example is a 'Received for shipment' bill as opposed to an 'On board' bill which is preferable since the foreign buyer is assured that the ship cannot sail without the cargo. However, both are valid documents of title to goods.

Dock warrants and warehouse warrants

These were some years ago in common usage as documents of title to goods discharged from a ship and left temporarily on the dock-side or in a statutory dock-side warehouse. They were freely transferable by endorsement and delivery but, being a right to claim goods and not money, they were not negotiable. The goods, resting at the port, could have been sold by mere delivery of the document of title, the buyer claiming the goods by production of the warrant.

In recent years these documents appear to have become obsolete in modern port usage. There is no trace today of the use of the dock warrant and there is only an isolated case of the use of the warehouse warrant in the Port of London. These documents, being transferable subject to defects in title, were of course quasi-negotiable.

American share certificates

This type of share certificate used extensively in the USA and Canada is on its face very similar to the English style of share certificate bearing the name of the registered holder in the normal way. But there is one main point of difference. A shareholding in an English company is transferred usually by the use of a separate document of transfer together with the certificate. The transfer is registered with the registrar of the company and a new certificate obtained in the name of the transferee. It will be remembered that it was because of the necessity for a separate document of transfer that we placed these share certificates in the class of 'assignable' documents.

With the American type, however, no separate document of transfer is necessary since this is already printed on the reverse of the certificate. The registered holder, desiring to transfer the shares, simply completes this form of transfer by inserting the name of the transferee and adding his own signature. The transferee will then forward the certificate to the company and exchange it for one in his own name. If, however, the registered holder does not insert the name of the transferee in the transfer form on the reverse but merely appends his signature, any subsequent holder can then insert his name, register the transfer with the company and become the registered holder of the shares. But until a holder does this, the certificate, thus endorsed in blank, would be transferable by mere delivery like bearer bonds. This ability to transfer by delivery is a characteristic of the negotiable instrument. But the bearer of an American-type share certificate indorsed in blank in this way cannot sue on the instrument in his own name. He must complete the transfer form and register himself as the new owner before this is possible. Consequently this type of share certificate is not fully negotiable.

IOUs

These documents have only the shadow of the characteristics of the negotiable instrument. They contain an admission of debt and with it an *implied* undertaking that payment of the debt will be made sometime (note—if it was a *written* undertaking to repay at some date, the document would be a promissory note). However, the debt of which the IOU is evidence is assignable under the Law of Property Act 1925, and, as the IOU would doubtless be handed to the assignee if the debt were assigned, it bears a little resemblance to a transferable or assignable instrument. Consequently, some authorities include the IOU in the category of quasi-negotiable instruments. This, though, is very debatable, since the document itself is merely ancillary to an assignment of the real debt.

Part 2
Bills of Exchange Act 1882

Preliminary note

In the study of this Act, it should always be remembered that cheques are bills of exchange though all bills of exchange are not necessarily cheques. Except where otherwise stated, the provisions of this Act concerning bills of exchange apply equally to promissory notes.

The bill of exchange was one of the first choses in action to be accepted as negotiable. Its early use was for the settlement of debts between English and foreign merchants. Prior to the introduction of the bill of exchange, merchants were forced to send gold and silver, risking loss by shipwreck or theft. Between England and France there was considerable trade and gold was continually moving in both directions across the Channel. Yet, if Hood of London owed £500 to Cassais of Paris and Duprez of Paris owed £500 to the same Hood of London, it was absurd for Duprez to ship the gold to Hood for Hood to ship it back to Cassais. By Duprez's paying £500 or its French equivalent to Cassais, both obligations were discharged. It was up to Hood to 'marry' the two transactions and he did it by sending instructions through Cassais to Duprez, ordering the latter to pay Cassais, his fellow townsman. These instructions were the forerunner of the bill of exchange. Sometimes the instructions were framed so that payment was ordered to be made on demand or sometimes at a future date. In the latter case, if such instructions had been sent to Paris, Cassais (to whom payment was to be made) on receiving the instructions or bill of exchange would take the bill to Duprez and ascertain if everything was in order. Duprez would confirm that such was the case and probably assure Cassais that payment would be made on the given date, i.e., Duprez would *accept* the liability and sign his acceptance on the bill itself. So Cassais would have presented the bill for 'acceptance' and Duprez would have 'accepted' the bill. On the due date Cassais would again present the bill, this time for payment, and Duprez would honour his acceptance and pay the bill. Thus, there are three parties to a bill:

(1) The party who sent the instructions or 'drew the bill' called the *drawer*.
(2) The party who is to receive payment, viz., the *payee*.
(3) The party ordered to pay or, in other words the party on whom the bill is drawn, viz., the *drawee*.

With the popularity of the cheque has come a decline in the use of other types of bills of exchange, but the same triangular characteristics obtain. Hood is now a merchant with money in his banking account (his bankers owe him the money he has deposited). If he wants to pay a creditor he draws a bill on his bank (a cheque) ordering payment to the creditor and sends the cheque to the creditor who presents it for payment. In just the same way as before, the person making the first move to discharge the existing obligation is the one who owes money and to whom money is owed. Hood owes money to his creditor, but the bank owes money to Hood. Hood is the drawer, the bank the drawee, and the creditor the payee.

The Act of 1882, therefore, is not merely a piece of legislation concerning bills of exchange that are no longer in popular use, but is also the statute governing a type of bill of exchange, which is today the currency of commerce, viz., the cheque.

Bills of Exchange Act 1882

Part 1

Preliminary [Sections 1–2]

1. Short title

This Act may be cited as the Bills of Exchange Act 1882.

2. Interpretation of terms

In this Act, unless the context otherwise requires:

'Acceptance' means an acceptance completed by delivery or notification.

'Action' includes counter-claim and set-off.

'Banker' includes a body of persons whether incorporated or not who carry on the business of banking.

'Bankrupt' includes any person whose estate is vested in a trustee or assignee under the law for the time being in force relating to bankruptcy.

'Bearer' means the person in possession of a bill or note which is payable to bearer.

'Bill' means bill of exchange, and 'note' means promissory note.

'Delivery' means transfer of possession, actual or constructive, from one person to another.

'Holder' means the payee or indorsee of a bill or note who is in possession of it, or the bearer thereof.

'Indorsement' means an indorsement completed by delivery.

'Issue' means the first delivery of a bill or note, complete in form to a person who takes it as a holder.

'Person' includes a body of persons whether incorporated or not.

'Value' means valuable consideration.
'Written' includes printed, and 'writing' includes print.

The terms 'Acceptance', 'Delivery', 'Indorsement', and 'Issue' are developed further in sections 17 to 21 below.

Bearer   Each bill states to whom the money is to be paid; otherwise it would not be a bill (see section 3). The payee, as he is called, can be indicated in three ways, e.g.:

(1) Pay James Brown or order (if the words 'or order' do not appear then they are nevertheless deemed to be there unless there are words on the bill prohibiting its transfer—see section 8).
(2) Pay James Brown or bearer.
(3) Pay bearer.

The effect of (2) and (3) is to order payment to whoever is in possession of the bill. In (2) the name James Brown can be ignored, and the bill is payable to bearer just as in (3). Such bills are called 'bearer bills' and anyone in possession of such a bill is called 'the bearer'. Mark, however, that to be a bearer, a person must be in possession of a BEARER bill. The everyday use of the word 'bearer' is not so narrow as this. I might send a note round to my neighbour as follows: 'I would like you to return my lawn-mower—kindly hand to bearer'. That is everyday usage of the word meaning a person delivering a document or letter, etc. But it is *not* the Bills of Exchange Act usage and the word 'bearer' must be used only in its narrow sense, viz., a person in possession of no other bill but a BEARER bill.

In (1) where payment is directed to be made to James Brown or order, we have an ORDER bill and until James Brown transfers it to someone else (as he can since it is a negotiable instrument) it is payable only to J Brown. If he wishes to negotiate it to W Smith, he will write on the back (i.e., indorse it) 'Pay W Smith or order' and add his signature 'J Brown' (see section 31). It is then payable only to W Smith until such a time as Smith similarly transfers it. The indorsement of Brown is known as a special indorsement since he indorses it specially to Smith (see section 34). But Brown is not obliged to write the words 'Pay W Smith'. The simple signature 'J Brown' as an indorsement is quite sufficient to transfer the bill (see 'Deliverable state', p. 22 above), but this simple indorsement (or, as it is called, 'indorsement in blank') would render the bill payable to anyone who possessed it, i.e., *it would be thence-forward payable to bearer*. Thus, to sum up, a bearer bill is one that is expressed to be payable to bearer or an order bill that has been indorsed in blank, and both are transferable by mere delivery. What is the difference? In effect, none, but it should be observed that whilst the former will always be payable to bearer no matter how many times it is transferred, the latter can be reconverted to an ORDER bill by a subsequent special indorsement. (A special indorsement on the former type would, of course, have no effect whatever).

The holder   This person is, as the section says, 'the payee or indorsee of a bill who is in possession of it, or the bearer thereof'. We can quickly dispose of the last few words 'or the bearer thereof'. We have seen above who 'a bearer' is. Now we see that, besides being a person in possession of a bearer bill, he is also *always the holder of it*.

The first part of the definition of a holder concerns order bills and we see that if the payee or an indorsee of an order bill has the bill in his possession, he is the holder. What, then is the payee or indorsee? The payee, as we have already seen, is that person whose name appears on the face of the bill as the person to whom payment is to be made. Thus we saw that a bill can be drawn payable as follows: 'Pay James Brown or order' and that Brown is the payee. Also we found that Brown could transfer the bill specially to Smith by a special indorsement, viz., by writing on the back 'Pay W Smith or order—J Brown' and that thenceforward it would be payable to Smith. Now, although the money is then to be paid to Smith, the latter is *not* the new payee—there is no such thing. A bill is issued in the first place to the payee and subsequently by transfers (with special indorsements) it goes to first indorsee, second indorsee and so on.

The true owner   Regarding bearer bills we observe that a person who finds or steals a bearer bill is nevertheless the holder of it, since he is the person in possession of a bill payable to bearer. But he is not the lawful owner of it since the bill belongs to the person, who lost it, viz., the true owner. Consequently, although there can be only one holder of a bill at any given moment (since it can be in possession of only one person at a time) there can be at one and the same time, in some circumstances, a person who is the holder and another person who is the true owner. The latter will, of course, have every right to sue the former for the return of his bill. But if the thief, before he is discovered, negotiates the bill to a *bona fide* transferee for value, then the latter will become both the holder and the true owner, defeating all the claims of the original true owner. In normal cases, however, where there has been no theft, fraud, or anything to render the holder's title defective, the bearer (of a BEARER bill) or the payee or indorsee of an order bill will be both the holder and the true owner (see section 29).

A person may find, however, that the bill contains a forged signature and his claims to be a holder may consequently fail. This is the case with both bearer and order bills on which the drawer's signature has been forged, and also in the case of order bills where an indorsement has been forged. This is dealt with fully under section 24 and it is recommended that this section and section 29 be studied next before proceeding to section 3.

Part II

Bills of exchange [Sections 3–72]

Form and Interpretation. [Sections 3–21]

3. Bill of exchange defined

(1) A bill of exchange is an unconditional order in writing, addressed by one person to another, signed by the person giving it, requiring the person to whom it is addressed to pay on demand or at a fixed or determinable future time a sum certain in money to or to the order of a specified person, or to bearer.

(2) An instrument which does not comply with these conditions, or which orders any act to be done in addition to the payment of money, is not a bill of exchange.

(3) An order to pay out of a particular fund is not unconditional within the meaning of this section; but an unqualified order to pay, coupled with (a) an indication of a particular fund out of which the drawee is to reimburse himself or a particular account to be debited with the amount, or (b) a statement of the transaction which gives rise to the bill, is unconditional.

(4) A bill is not invalid by reason:

(a) That it is not dated;

(b) That it does not specify the value given, or that any value has been given therefor;

(c) That it does not specify the place where it is drawn or the place where it is payable.

The definition of a bill in subsection (1) must be analysed.

Unconditional order

The bill must be an *order* to pay and consequently, a mere request is not sufficient. This does not rule out the use of politeness. The words 'Please pay' fulfil the requirements and are considered to be just as much an order as the abrupt word 'Pay'. But the words 'I should be pleased if you would kindly pay' would be considered as a mere request and not an order.

Specimen bill

£900   Nottingham
                                                             1 Jan 1983
                        Ninety days after date pay to Edwin
                        & Co Ltd, or order the sum of Nine
                        hundred pounds for value received.
                                                          John Hedley

        To Mr John Robins,
            High Street,
                Winchester

The order must be unconditional; i.e. it must be entirely unqualified. The order to pay must not depend upon a certain thing happening or some circumstances obtaining at the time of payment or the performance of some act. For example, a document containing 'If your new play at Drury Lane is a success, pay on demand to John Smith or order the sum of £20' is not a valid bill since payment is conditional upon the success of a play. Again, 'Please pay on demand £100 to John Bull providing the goods he supplies are up to standard' is not the wording of a valid bill. These examples are fairly obvious. Now read subsection (3) of this section. From this we see that an order to pay out of a particular fund is also a conditional order, yet a simple unqualified order to pay coupled with a direction to debit a certain account (or containing a direction for re-imbursement) is unconditional. For example, an order containing 'Pay £1,000 out of the proceeds of sale of my farm at Haslemere' is not a valid bill. Why has the framer of this Act made this proviso? Simply because of the difficulty that would arise if the proceeds of sale did not amount to £1,000. Again, if I drew an order as follows 'Pay from my No. 2 account to Mary Maltby the sum of £10', it would not be a valid bill since it is an order to pay from a particular fund, yet if the document is drawn 'Pay Mary Maltby the sum of £10 and debit my No. 2 account' it is quite a valid bill, since the additional words merely indicate the account to be debited. The distinction is not so subtle as might at first appear. In case of doubt it is advisable to consider which of the following the instrument resembles:

(1) Pay £100 from my No. 2 A/c.
(2) Pay £100 and charge to my No. 2 A/c.

It is quite normal for a customer of a bank to operate more than one account. Cheques are often seen marked 'No. 2 A/c.' and they are quite valid bills of exchange falling into category (2) above.

Before leaving the question of conditional orders, it should be observed that although a bill to be valid must order unconditional payment, a bill can be accepted conditionally or indorsed conditionally and yet remain a valid bill (see sections 19 and 33).

Writing   The order must be in 'writing' and this, as section 2 says, includes typewriting and printing. Apparently ink is not the only medium insisted on and, therefore, a bill drawn up in pencil is valid. The Act does not state maximum and minimum sizes of the document or that writing must be on paper or parchment only. (Therefore, as the late Sir Alan Herbert humorously pointed out, the order to pay could be written on the white belly of a live cow which if properly signed would be a valid bill!!) The drawing of cheques in pencil is not encouraged by banks owing to the easy opportunity for fraudulent alteration.

Addressed by one person to another   The person addressing the order, i.e., giving the order, is called the DRAWER of the bill (he draws up the document). The person to whom the order is given is known as the DRAWEE and regarding him, sections 5 and 6 should be perused later. Where the bill is not payable on demand but at some future date, and the drawee meanwhile agrees to pay on the due date and signs the bill expressing his agreement, he is thereafter called the 'Acceptor'.

An acceptance of a bill of exchange

J. Robins

£900 Nottingham
1 Jan 1983

Ninety days after date pay to Edwin & Co Ltd, or order, the sum of nine hundred pounds for value received.

John Hedley

To Mr John Robins,
High Street,
Winchester

The bill is now referred to as an acceptance.

Signed by the person giving the order (i.e., signed by the drawer) If the order is not signed by him then it is not a valid bill. (If it is signed *for* him by some authorised person then this operates as the drawer's signature, e.g., 'Per pro James Harrison, R. Johns, attorney'. But if it is signed on behalf of the drawer by someone having no authority to do so, or if the drawer's signature is forged then the bill cannot be considered signed by the drawer. (See section 24.)

Requiring the drawee to pay on demand or at a fixed or determinable future date . . . What is meant by 'payable on demand' is explained in section 10 and what is meant by a 'fixed or determinable future date' is considered under sections 11–14.

A sum certain in money This is explained under section 9.

To or to the order of a specified person or to bearer This means that a bill must be payable to:
(a) A specified person (e.g., 'Pay J Smith'), or
(b) The order of a specified person (e.g., 'Pay the order of John Smith' or 'Pay John Smith or order') or
(c) Bearer (e.g., 'Pay bearer', 'Pay John Smith or bearer').

The matter is dealt with further under section 7.

It is important to note that unless the order fulfils all the requirements of section 3(1), it cannot be a valid bill. What happens then, if a person gives value for an instrument that for some reason or other is not a valid bill? Does he lose his money? Not necessarily. We have seen that a bill of exchange is a special kind of chose in action. If an instrument does not entirely fulfil the requirements of section 3(1), it may still be a chose in action (though not a bill) on which there will be a party liable. A person giving value for the instrument will probably be an assignee of the chose in action, if such it is, and sue the party liable on the instrument. For example, an instrument ordering delivery of goods is not a bill since it is not an order to pay a sum certain in money; it is not negotiable but it *is* a chose in action, and the assignee can obtain the goods represented in the instrument by action at law, if necessary.

4. Inland and foreign bills

(1) An inland bill is a bill which is or on the face of it purports to be (a) both drawn and payable within the British Islands, or (b) drawn within the British Islands upon some person resident therein. Any other bill is a foreign bill.

For the purposes of this Act 'British Islands' mean any part of the United Kingdom of Great Britain and Ireland, the islands of Man, Guernsey, Jersey, Alderney, and Sark, and the islands adjacent to any of them being part of the dominions of Her Majesty.

(2) Unless the contrary appear on the face of the bill the holder may treat it as an inland bill.

This section is self-explanatory. But why is this distinction necessary? Later, under section 51, we shall see what steps a holder of a bill should take if his bill is dishonoured, and it will be seen that the action he takes will depend to some extent on whether the bill is an inland one or a foreign one. So we must distinguish between the two from the outset.

5. Effect where different parties to bill are the same person

(1) A bill may be drawn payable to, or to the order of, the drawer; or it may be drawn payable to, or to the order of, the drawee.

(2) Where in a bill drawer and drawee are the same person, or where the drawee is a fictious person or a person not having capacity to contract, the holder may treat the instrument, at his option, either as a bill of exchange or as a promissory note.

Let us take this step by step.

(1) A bill may be drawn payable to, or to the order of the drawer, i.e., the payee and the drawer will be the same person.

A large number of bills, including cheques, are drawn thus. Such a bill would appear, for example, as follows:

```
£100                          Leeds
                              1 Jan 1983
              Thirty days after date, pay to me
              or my order the sum of one hun-
              dred pounds.
                              J Smith

        To Lynton & Co,
           Mansfield
```

Such a bill could be used where J Smith had supplied goods to the value of £100 to Lynton & Co. He would require payment to be made to himself. Again, when a man requires money from his bank, he draws a cheque payable to 'Self'. In both examples the drawer and payee are the same person.

(2) It may be payable to, or to the order of, the drawee.

Here the drawer is ordering the drawee to pay himself. This may appear absurd at first sight. But a common example occurs in the use of cheques. A cheque, as section 73 below states, is a bill of exchange drawn on a banker payable on demand. The banker is the drawee. If your banker purchases stocks and shares for you, you will very probably pay your bank by cheque. The cheque will be drawn *on* the bank and payable *to* the bank —the payee and drawee will be one and the same person.

Subsection 2 of this section   How can the drawer and drawee be the same person? This situation arises where a branch of a business house draws a bill on its Head Office (e.g., a branch bank often issues a draft drawn on its Head Office and this is a banker's draft). Such instruments are not strictly valid bills since, under section 3, we observed that a bill must be drawn by one person *on another,* i.e., the drawer and drawee must be two separate persons. But this subsection states that the holder *can treat it as though it were a bill or,* if he so chooses, *treat it as though it were a promissory note.* So, the holder has all the rights that he would have normally with a valid bill. But there is one main point of difference. Where a valid bill is dishonoured, i.e., where the drawee refuses to accept or pay the bill, the holder can demand the money which the bill represents from any of the parties—viz., those who have signed the bill as drawer, acceptor or indorser—if necessary the holder can sue any or all in court. The more parties there are to look to, the more likelihood there is of getting the money. But if the holder finds that the drawer and drawee are the same person, it will mean that he has one party less to fall back on for payment in the event of dishonour than he would have had with a valid bill. The same circumstances arise where the drawee is a fictitious person or a person who cannot be sued in court (having no capacity to contract), e.g., a minor or a lunatic—(see section 41)—again, in such cases, there is one person less to sue than there normally is. This does not seem fair and accordingly the Act offers a little compensation and states in this section that the holder can treat the instrument as a promissory note if he wishes. Why is this offer compensation? Because, in the case of promissory notes, the holder, though not losing any of his usual *rights* that he possesses with a bill, is excused some of the *duties* attached to a holder of a bill. This is reviewed later in section 89(3).

6. Address to drawee

(1) The drawee must be named or otherwise indicated in a bill with reasonable certainty.

(2) A bill may be addressed to two or more drawees whether they are partners or not, but an order addressed to two drawees in the alternative or to two or more drawees in succession is not a bill of exchange.

This does not require much amplification. The Act requires *reasonable* certainty regarding the drawee. There appears nothing in the Act that makes the address of the drawee essential and what is reasonable certainty would be decided on by the facts of the individual case. For example, a cheque drawn on

'Barclays Bank, Ltd', with no branch specified is quite a valid cheque upon which all parties who have signed are liable if it should not be paid. Such a cheque should be presented at the Head Office of the bank, but payment would be refused if the relative account was not held there.

The reader should observe that although joint drawees are allowed, alternate drawees are not.

7. Certainty required as to payee

(1) Where a bill is not payable to bearer, the payee must be named or otherwise indicated therein with reasonable certainty.

(2) A bill may be made payable to two or more payees jointly, or it may be made payable in the alternative to one of two, or one or some of several payees. A bill may also be made payable to the holder of an office for the time being.

(3) Where the payee is a fictitious or non-existing person the bill may be treated as payable to bearer.

As with the case of the drawee, so the payee of a bill must be indicated with reasonable certainty. Again, what is reasonable certainty will be decided by the facts of each case. The payee's *full* name is not insisted on nor is his address. Thus, a bill payable to J Smith is quite valid though there be thousands of people by such a name. The mere name of the payee is sufficient and that is all that nearly every cheque ever gives for the payee's indication. Joint payees are permitted and also alternate payees (whereas alternate *drawees*, we saw in section 6, are not permitted). But if you have joint payees, each one must be indicated with reasonable certainty. Thus a bill payable to 'H Jones and another' is not a valid bill (though, in spite of this, such a manner of indicating joint payees is commonly used by companies in the payment of dividends).

A bill may be drawn payable to the holder of an office for the time being. Thus a cheque is quite in order if it is drawn payable to 'The City Treasurer', 'Collector of Taxes', 'Secretary of Brumpton Tennis Club', etc., etc.

Subsection 3 requires considerable investigation. 'Where the payee is a fictitious or non-existing person the bill may be treated as payable to bearer'.

The framers of the Act, however, omitted to state what they meant by a fictitious or a non-existing payee and it was left for the courts to decide subsequently. The courts have decided that a fictitious person is *not* the same as a non-existing person, and to determine whether a payee is:

(a) existing; or
(b) non-existing; or
(c) fictitious;

the court rules that it is essential to find what was in the drawer's mind when he signed the bill.

Existing payee   If the drawer knew of the existence of the payee at the time he signed the bill and intended the payee to receive payment then the payee is existing.

Non-existing payee   If it is found that the drawer did not know of the existence of the payee when he signed, then the payee is a non-existing person notwithstanding that there was then an actual living person of that name. This was the decision in the case of *Clutton v Attenborough* (1897). A dishonest clerk had induced his employer to sign cheques payable to a person named Brett, by saying that money was owing to Brett. There were, however, no such debts and the drawer had never heard of anyone of that name. Thus, although the drawer apparently intended payment to be made to Brett he did not know of the existence of any such person (though there were plenty of persons in England named Brett) and the Court thus ruled that the payee was non-existing and the cheques payable to bearer.

Fictitious payee   On the other hand, if the drawer *is* aware of the existence of the payee but does not intend him to receive payment, then the payee is deemed to be fictitious. This was the ruling in *Bank of England v Vagliano* (1891). Vagliano's clerk obtained the acceptance of his employer to spurious bills, which appeared to have been drawn by Vagliano's customers on Vagliano payable to someone known to Vagliano, but were in fact forgeries of the clerk. The clerk forged the payee's indorsement in each case and obtained the money. The court held that the real drawer of the bills was the clerk who forged them, and he knew of the existence of the payees but did not intend them to receive payment. The payees were accordingly considered fictitious and the 'bills' payable to bearer.

The importance of these decisions is not easily seen. Let us take the case of *Clutton v Attenborough*. The clerk induced the employer to sign the cheques. Afterwards he forged the payees' indorsements and transferred some of the cheques for value to Attenborough, who cashed them. When the fraud was discovered, Clutton sued Attenborough for the money he had obtained. Now, although Attenborough was a *bona fide* transferee for value, the forgery by Brett of a vital indorsement (the payee's) would normally have upset his claim to a good title to a cheque payable to order (see section 24) and he would have been compelled to refund to Clutton. But the court ruled that the payees were non-existing and the cheques were, therefore, payable to bearer. Since indorsements on cheques drawn to bearer can be ignored whether genuine or forged, Attenborough's title to the cheques was established since he had been the *bona fide* transferee for value of bearer cheques (see section 29).

Impersonal payees   Under section 3, we saw that a bill must be payable to or to the order of a specified *person* or to bearer. Consequently documents drawn up as bills but with impersonal payees cannot be regarded as valid bills, and in dealing with them great care is required. For example, a 'cheque' payable to 'Wages or order' (a common usage with business men) is not payable to a *specified person*, not even a fictitious or non-existing person, and on no account should be treated as payable to bearer (*North & South Insurance Corpn v National Provincial Bank Ltd,* 1936.) It is very doubtful indeed whether such instruments are negotiable. However, the use of the impersonal payee seems to be confined in practice entirely to 'cheques' intended to be cashed at the drawee-bank counter, and by virtue of the Cheques Act 1957 (section 1(2)) and the ruling in *Orbit Mining & Trading Co Ltd v Westminster Bank Ltd* [1962] 3 All ER 565, bankers are placed in the same position, whether collecting or paying these instruments, as though they were valid cheques.

Finally it should be observed that the foregoing will not apply to a cheque payable to 'Wages or bearer', 'Income tax or bearer' since such cheques are bearer cheques (see section 2).

8. What bills are negotiable

(1) When a bill contains words prohibiting transfer, or indicating an intention that it should not be transferable, it is valid as between the parties thereto, but is not negotiable.

(2) A negotiable bill may be payable either to order or to bearer.

(3) A bill is payable to bearer which is expressed to be so payable, or on which the only or last indorsement is an indorsement in blank.

(4) A bill is payable to order which is expressed to be so payable, or which is expressed to be payable to a particular person, and does not contain words prohibiting transfer or indicating an intention that it should not be transferable.

(5) Where a bill, either originally or by indorsement, is expressed to be payable to the order of a specified person, and not to him or his order, it is nevertheless payable to him or his order at his option.

Subsection (1)   Examples of this are bills drawn as follows:
(a) 'Pay John Davids only';
(b) 'Pay John Davids not transferable';
(c) 'Pay John Davids' with the words 'not transferable' appearing anywhere on the face of the bill.

Obviously such bills, being non-transferable, cannot be negotiable since negotiability implies, amongst other things, absolute freedom of transfer. They are, however, valid contracts. Thus a bill drawn by J Bull payable to 'John Davids only' and accepted by William Smith is a valid contract between these three persons, and Davids, with the bill in his possession, can enforce payment against Smith or Bull. But the liability of the acceptor and drawer is limited only to the payee, and should the latter transfer the bill to a fourth party the latter would have no right to sue the drawer or acceptor *in his own name* but would have to get the payee, Davids, to sue for him. The law of equity would if need be compel Davids to do this. In fact, such a transferee would be in the same position as was a transferee of a chose in action prior to 1873 (see p. 10).

Except for crossed cheques, the Act makes no provision for

bills crossed 'not negotiable', since in any case a crossing on a bill other than a cheque is completely ineffective. In the case of *Hibernian Bank v Gysin and Hanson* (1938), it was held that if the words 'Not negotiable' did appear on a bill other than a cheque, then they were to be considered as rendering the bill not transferable. But a *crossed cheque* marked 'Not negotiable' *is* freely transferable but not with all the characteristics of negotiability, i.e. it is transferable subject to any existing equities like a bill of lading (see section 81).

Subsection (2) 'A negotiable bill may be payable either to order or to bearer'.
   This is apparent from our study of section 2 of the Act.

Subsection (3) 'A bill is payable to bearer which is expressed to be so payable or on which the only or last indorsement is in blank'.
   This was also dealt with in studying section 2.

Subsection (4) 'A bill is payable to order which is expressed to be so payable, or which is expressed to be payable to a particular person and does not contain words prohibiting transfer or indicating an intention that it should not be transferable'.
   Here is the authority for what was stated regarding order bills in the review of section 2. Thus a bill drawn 'Pay John Smith' is an order bill as though it were drawn 'Pay John Smith or order' providing there is nothing to indicate that the bill is not transferable. The words 'or order' are presumed if not written since a bill, being fully negotiable, can be transferred by the payee to any transferee he 'orders', (i.e., by indorsing it and adding to the indorsement such words as 'pay John Thomas').
   Whilst on the subject of order and bearer bills it is worth recalling that a bill drawn originally to bearer (as distinct from an order bill endorsed in blank) must have the word 'bearer' on the face of the bill, e.g., 'Pay bearer', 'Pay J Smith or bearer'. Where you have a cheque drawn 'Pay J Smith or order', with the words 'or order' struck out and the alteration initialled by the drawer, it is commonly thought that such a cheque is payable to bearer. This is not so. Such a cheque is read as 'Pay J Smith' and, unless there are further words to indicate that the cheque is not transferable, the cheque remains transferable and the words 'or order' are implied under this subsection even though they have been deliberately struck out!

Subsection (5) 'Where a bill, either originally or by indorsement, is expressed to be payable to the order of a specified person, and not to him or his order, it is nevertheless payable to him or his order at his option.'

It is not unusual to see a bill drawn 'Pay to the order of J Smith.' To interpret this literally, one might conclude that payment was to be made *not* to J Smith but to someone else he indicates to receive payment (i.e., his order). This subsection provides, however, that such wording can also be read as 'Pay J Smith or order' if the payee wishes.

9. Sum payable

(1) The sum payable by a bill is a sum certain within the meaning of this Act, although it was required to be paid:
(a) With interest;
(b) By stated instalments;
(c) By stated instalments, with a provision that upon default in payment of any instalment the whole shall become due;
(d) According to an indicated rate of exchange or according to a rate of exchange to be ascertained as directed by the bill.

(2) Where the sum payable is expressed in words and also in figures, and there is a discrepancy between the two, the sum denoted by the words is the amount payable.

(3) Where a bill is expressed to be payable with interest, unless the instrument otherwise provides, interest runs from the date of the bill, and if the bill is undated from the issue thereof.

It will be remembered that section 3, in defining a valid bill, stated that it must order the payment of a sum *certain in money*, i.e., a sum at any time capable of being calculated or ascertained. Examples of the most simple form of a sum certain in money are '£50' or '$10'. But this section provides that a sum is equally certain if it is to be paid with interest, or by instalments, or according to an indicated or ascertainable rate of exchange (where the sum is in foreign currency). But it is imperative that the amount shall be capable of exact calculation. For instance, if a bill is drawn payable with interest, without expressing the relative rate of interest, it will be invalid since the sum is not certain.

Subsection (1)(d) covers a common practice in our export trade where bills are drawn in sterling on foreign importers and the equivalent amount of the importer's currency due is indicated by stating the rate of exchange on the bill or by ordering that payment shall be made at a certain rate of exchange to be advised to him on the due date of the bill. Conversely, bills are often drawn abroad in foreign currency on English importers. In such cases, the amount of sterling that will discharge the bill should be calculated, in the absence of other directions, at the rate of exchange ruling on the date of payment (see section 72(4)). The offer of payment in notes, etc., of the currency concerned could be refused on the grounds that in England (where the English importer is paying the bill) such currency is not legal tender.

No section of the Act requires the sum payable to be in both words and figures. Consequently, a bill is valid if it merely bears the amount in figures, dangerous though such a practice may be in facilitating unauthorised alteration.

Should the amount be expressed in both words and figures and there is a discrepancy between the two, the sum payable is the amount in words. Consequently, a banker, on being presented with such a cheque for payment, would be in order to pay the amount in words, though he is entitled to return the cheque marked 'words and figures differ' since he has the right to demand from his customers that their cheques be drawn in clear and unambiguous terms.

10. Bill payable on demand

(1) A bill is payable on demand:

(a) Which is expressed to be payable on demand, or at sight, or on presentation; or

(b) In which no time for payment was expressed.

(2) Where a bill is accepted or indorsed when it is overdue, it shall, as regards the acceptor who so accepts, or any indorser who so indorses it, be deemed a bill payable on demand.

Subsection (1) is self-explanatory.

An example of subsection (2) is as follows. A bill dated 1 March drawn payable 30 days after date is due and payable on

31 March. Anyone who takes the bill on or after that date can treat it as a demand bill.

11. Bill payable at a future time

A bill is payable at a determinable future time within the meaning of this Act which is expressed to be payable:

(1) At a fixed period after date or sight;
(2) On or at a fixed period after the occurrence of a specified event which is certain to happen, though the time of happening may be uncertain.

An instrument expressed to be payable on a contingency is not a bill, and the happening of the event does not cure the defect.

Example of bill payable after date

£400   London
                                            31 Mar 1983
              30 days after date pay to the order of
              Lloyds Bank Ltd, the sum of four
              hundred pounds.
                                            William Rowe

To Messrs Raymond Green & Co,
       Leicester

This bill is payable 30 days after 31 March, viz., 30 April.

Example of bill payable after sight

£125   Manchester
                                            30 Mar 1983
              30 days after sight pay to me or my
              order the sum of one hundred and
              twenty-five pounds for value received.
                                            Roger Fogg

To R Macdonald,
      Derby

'Sight' here means the first 'sighting' of the bill by the drawee

Macdonald. Although the bill is dated 30 March, it may not be seen by Macdonald, the drawee, until 10 April when presentation is made to him for his acceptance. In that case the due date of the bill would be 30 days after 10 April, viz. 10 May.

The method of calculation of due dates is studied under section 14.

Subsection (2)   This validates a bill drawn with words such as 'On the death of Prince Philip, pay to me or my order, etc., etc.' The death of a living man is an inevitable and certain future event although the actual date cannot be ascertained beforehand. But a bill payable on the marriage of someone is invalid since it may never occur—it is a contingency as the Act says, and even the happening of the event will not validate the bill.

Likewise, a bill drawn payable at a fixed period after acceptance is not a legal bill since the drawee's acceptance is not a certain future event (*Korea Exchange Bank v Debenhams (Central Buying) Ltd* (1979) 123 Sol Jo 163, CA).

12. Omission of date in bill payable after date

Where a bill expressed to be payable at a fixed period after date is issued undated, or where the acceptance of a bill payable at a fixed period after sight is undated, any holder may insert therein the true date of issue or acceptance, and the bill shall be payable accordingly.

Provided that (1) where the holder in good faith and by mistake inserts a wrong date, and (2) in every case where a wrong date is inserted, if the bill subsequently comes into the hands of a holder in due course the bill shall not be avoided thereby, but shall operate and be payable as if the date so inserted had been the true date.

From section 11, it will be seen that where a bill is payable at a certain period after date, the date of the bill is vitally important in order to calculate the due date (although a bill is not invalid by being issued undated), and where it is payable at a period after sight the date of the drawee's 'sighting' is similarly essential for determining the due date. So the Act provides that any holder may insert the true date—more important too is that if the wrong date is inserted and the bill subsequently comes into the hands of a *bona fide* transferee for value, i.e. a holder in due course (see section 29), the inserted date will be treated as the correct date. Why is this important? An example will best explain.

Section 45 states that a bill must be presented for payment on the date it falls due, otherwise the drawer and indorsers are discharged from liability thereon. If a bill was due for payment 30 days after sighting and acceptance on 1 March, viz., on 31 March, then, failure to present the bill to the acceptor for payment on that date would discharge all previous parties to the bill (except the acceptor), even though the date of sighting or acceptance had not been placed on the bill. But if someone had inserted the date of sighting and acceptance as 11 March, then the holder of the bill would naturally present it to the acceptor for payment on 10 April. The delay of 10 days would be ignored *if the holder were a holder in due course*, and the drawer and indorsers would NOT be discharged from liability, since the date of sighting wrongly inserted would operate for the benefit of the holder in due course as the true date.

13. Ante-dating and post-dating
(1) Where a bill or an acceptance or any indorsement on a bill is dated, the date shall, unless the contrary be proved, be deemed to be the true date of the drawing, acceptance, or indorsement, as the case may be.

(2) A bill is not invalid by reason only that it is ante-dated or post-dated, or that it bears date on a Sunday.

This section is fairly obvious. It is interesting to observe too, that a post-dated cheque, although a valid bill, is not strictly payable on demand since a banker would not pay it before that date. To do so would be incurring unnecessary risk, for the drawer has every right to countermand payment (i.e., 'stop the cheque') before the date of the cheque.

14. Computation of time of payment
Where a bill is not payable on demand the day on which it falls due is determined as follows:

(1) The bill is due and payable in all cases on the last day of the time of payment as fixed by the bill or, if that is a non-business day, on the succeeding business day.

The original subsection (1) was replaced by the Banking and Financial Dealings Act 1971.

(2) Where a bill is payable at a fixed period after date, after sight, or after the happening of a specified event, the time of payment is determined by excluding the day from which the time is to begin to run and by including the day of payment.

(3) Where a bill is payable at a fixed period after sight, the time begins to run from the date of the acceptance if the bill be accepted, and from the date of noting or protest if the bill be noted or protested for non-acceptance, or for non-delivery.

(4) The term 'month' in a bill means calendar month.

The due date of a bill is indicated by the provisions of this section which are fairly clear. The student should note:

(a) Months are *calendar* months. Thus, one month after February 29th is March 29th NOT March 31st, and a month after January 31st is February 28th (or 29th in leap years); the fact that February is a short month is ignored.

(b) The period for which a bill is drawn is often called its 'usance'.

(c) Subsection (3) is important. The due date of a bill payable after sight is calculated from the date of sighting which generally is the date of acceptance also. It may happen, however, that the drawee refuses to accept the bill. If so, the holder may note or protest the bill for non-acceptance as soon as possible, and then the due date is calculated from the date the noting or protesting was made (for noting the protesting see section 51). But if, after all this, the drawee subsequently accepts then, according to section 18(3) the holder has the right to insist on the acceptance being dated as at the date of the first presentation.

(d) Distinguish between a 'sight bill' (i.e., a bill payable at sight) and a bill payable *after* sight. The former is payable at sight (or on demand) whereas the latter is payable on a date *subsequent* to the sighting (the date being calculated in accordance with the terms of the bill).

15. Case of need
The drawer of a bill and any indorser may insert therein the

name of a person to whom the holder may resort in case of need, that is to say, in case the bill is dishonoured by non-acceptance or non-payment. Such person is called the referee in case of need. It is in the option of the holder to resort to the referee in case of need or not as he may think fit.

It should be observed that there is no compulsion on the holder to refer the bill to the 'referee in case of need' if the bill is dishonoured, nor need the referee accept or pay the bill unless he so chooses. The name of a referee (that is, the person to whom you refer) is sometimes inserted by the drawer to avoid all the protracted actions that normally occur after the dishonour of a bill (dishonour being the refusal of the drawee to accept or his refusal to pay). After all, if the drawee refuses to accept or pay the bill, the drawer is then primarily liable for payment as he issued the bill. If he can arrange for acceptance and/or payment to be made by (say) an agent should the drawee dishonour the bill, it can save a lot of trouble. (See 'acceptance for honour' and 'payment for honour' under sections 65 to 68).

This is particularly useful in the case of bills payable abroad. When goods are exported from England to, say, Hong Kong a bill of lading is obtained by the English exporter who draws a bill of exchange on the Hong Kong importer and attaches the bill of lading to the bill of exchange. These documents are sent to Hong Kong through a bank and the importer, by accepting or paying the bill of exchange, obtains the bill of lading which can be exchanged for the goods when the ship docks at Hong Kong. If the importer fails to accept and/or pay the bill of exchange, a referee in case of need (usually an agent of the English exporter) can then intervene by accepting and/or paying the bill, obtain control of the goods and dispose of them locally. The alternative would be the return of the goods to England with the attendant costly freight charges.

16. Optional stipulations by drawer or indorser
The drawer of a bill, and any indorser, may insert therein an express stipulation:
    (1) Negativing or limiting his own liability to the holder;
    (2) Waiving as regards himself some or all of the holder's duties.

Negativing or limiting liability to the holder   This occurs, for
example, when a party adds to his signature the words '*sans recours*'
or 'without recourse to me'. He means that, should the bill be dishonoured, the holder cannot look to him for repayment—a liability which he normally incurs when he signs the bill as drawer or
indorser. One might well ask why a person should be allowed so
easily to avoid the liability that every party normally incurs. There
is only one answer. If Brown has a cheque for £100 payable to him
and he persuades Smith to give him £100 in bank notes for it,
Brown must indorse the cheque before he transfers it to Smith. If
Smith foolishly allows Brown to indorse in this way, avoiding liability on the cheque, then it is his concern.

A drawee banker paying such a cheque can ignore the words.

The reader is advised to refer to section 58 at this juncture.

Waiving as regards himself some or all of the holder's duties   If a
bill is dishonoured then the holder must notify the dishonour to all
prior parties. Any prior party who fails to receive notice of dishonour will not be liable to the holder. If, however, John Smith
indorses a bill 'J Smith—notice of dishonour excused' before
negotiating it, he means that the holder need not advise him of dishonour if such should occur, and still agrees to remain liable on the
bill.

17. Definition and requisites of acceptance
(1) The acceptance of a bill is the signification by the drawee
of his assent to the order of the drawer.

(2) An acceptance is invalid unless it complies with the
following conditions, namely:
- (a) It must be written on the bill and be signed by the
  drawee. The mere signature of the drawee without
  additional words is sufficient.
- (b) It must not express that the drawee will perform his
  promise by any other means than the payment of
  money.

It should be observed that the mere signature of the drawee is
quite sufficient and that when he has signed his acceptance he is
thenceforward known as the 'acceptor' and not the drawee and

is primarily liable for the payment of the bill. Generally, he will add the word 'accepted' and possibly the date—the latter is important if the bill is payable at a period after sight. He may also add such words as 'payable at Midland Bank, Blankton', and these words would indicate his desire and authority that his bankers should pay the bill on his behalf when it falls due and debit his account.

The acceptance is not normally complete, however, until the bill has been delivered (handed back) to the person who presents it for acceptance except as provided by section 21.

After acceptance by the drawee the bill itself is often called 'an acceptance'.

18. Time for acceptance
A bill may be accepted:

(1) Before it has been signed by the drawer, or while otherwise incomplete:

(2) When it is overdue, or after it has been dishonoured by a previous refusal to accept, or by non-payment;

(3) When a bill payable after sight is dishonoured by non-acceptance, and the drawee subsequently accepts it, the holder, in the absence of any different agreement, is entitled to have the bill accepted as of the date of first presentment to the drawee for acceptance.

Subsection (3), it will be seen, is an exception to section 14.

19. General and qualified acceptances
(1) An acceptance is either (a) general or (b) qualified.

(2) A general acceptance assents without qualification to the order of the drawer. A qualified acceptance in express terms varies the effect of the bill as drawn.

In particular, an acceptance is qualified which is:

(a) Conditional, that is to say, which makes payment by the acceptor dependent on the fulfilment of a condition therein stated;

(b) Partial, that is to say, an acceptance to pay part only of the amount for which the bill is drawn;

(c) Local, that is to say, an acceptance to pay only at a particular specified place;
    An acceptance to pay at a particular place is a general acceptance, unless it expressly states that the bill is to be paid there only and not elsewhere;
(d) Qualified as to time;
(e) The acceptance of some one or more of the drawees, but not of all.

A general acceptance would, therefore, be either:
(1) Mere signature of the drawee;
(2) Signature of the drawee plus the word 'accepted';
(3) Signature of the drawee plus the date;
(4) Signature of the drawee plus the word 'accepted' and the date.
(5) Any of (1)–(4) plus such words as 'Payable at Lloyds Bank, Blankton'.

Examples of qualified acceptances
(a) *Conditional* 'Accepted payable providing goods are up to Board of Trade standards.'
(b) *Partial* 'Accepted for £80 only' (where bill is for £100).
(c) *Local* 'Accepted payable at Lloyd's Bank, Blankton only' (without the word 'only' it would be a general acceptance).
(d) *Qualified as to time* 'Accepted payable at six months after date' (where the bill is drawn at three months after date).
(e) *Acceptance by some but not all of the drawees* Section 6 states that a bill can be drawn on joint drawees. If a bill was drawn on four people jointly and only three consented to accept then their acceptance, if taken, would be a qualified one.
    It is strongly recommended that section 44 be studied at this stage.

20. Inchoate instruments
(1) Where a simple signature on a blank paper is delivered by the signer in order that it may be converted into a bill, it operates as a *prima facie* authority to fill it up as a complete bill for any amount, using the signature for that of the

drawer, or the acceptor, or an indorser; and, in like manner, when a bill is wanting in any material particular, the person in possession of it has a *prima facie* authority to fill up the omission in any way he thinks fit.

(2) In order that any such instrument when completed may be enforceable against any person who became a party thereto prior to its completion, it must be filled up within a reasonable time, and strictly in accordance with the authority given. Reasonable time for this purpose is a question of fact.

Provided that if any such instrument after completion is negotiated to a holder in due course it shall be valid and effectual for all purposes in his hands, and he may enforce it as if it had been filled up within a reasonable time and strictly in accordance with the authority given.

An inchoate bill is one lacking some material particular, e.g. a cheque with no amount stated, payee's name omitted, etc. (but a bill without the date of the drawing is *not* inchoate since the date is not essential to validity—see section 3(4)). Any person in possession of an inchoate bill has *prima facie* authority (i.e. the authority is presumed unless it can be proved otherwise) to complete the bill in any way he wishes but in order to bind the prior parties it must be completed within a reasonable time and strictly in accordance with the authority given. For example, it is not uncommon for a postal buyer of advertised goods to send his cheque to the advertising firm without completing the cheque as to the amount, requesting the sellers to complete it for the amount due. Where there is some doubt as to the precise amount due such an action is reasonable. A fraudulent seller could quite easily complete the cheque for a greater figure and negotiate it to an innocent third party who would be able to hold the drawer liable for the swollen amount.

Vital to this section are the opening words 'Where a simple signature on a blank paper *is delivered* . . .'. Thus the section operates only when delivery for the purpose of completion has in fact been made. If the drawer can prove that he did *not* deliver the bill then he can escape liability even though the bill has come into the hands of a holder in due course. The conclusive presumption of a valid delivery by all prior parties in favour of a holder in due course is for delivery of *complete* bills. An example of such non-delivery would be seen when a signed incomplete cheque is left on a desk and later picked up by a dishonest clerk.

21. Delivery

(1) Every contract on a bill whether it be the drawer's, the acceptor's, or an indorser's, is incomplete and revocable, until delivery of the instrument in order to give effect thereto.

Provided that where an acceptance is written on a bill, and the drawee gives notice to or according to the directions of the person entitled to the bill that he has accepted it, the acceptance then becomes complete and irrevocable.

(2) As between immediate parties, and as regards a remote party other than a holder in due course, the delivery:

(a) in order to be effectual must be made either by or under the authority of the party drawing, accepting, or indorsing, as the case may be;

(b) may be shown to have been conditional or for a special purpose only, and, not for the purpose of transferring the property in the bill.

But if the bill be in the hands of a holder in due course a valid delivery of the bill by all parties prior to him so as to make them liable to him is conclusively presumed.

(3) Where a bill is no longer in the possession of a party who has signed it as drawer, acceptor, or indorser, a valid and unconditional delivery by him is presumed until the contrary is proved.

In the normal way, liability on a bill arises not by a simple signature but by the signature plus the delivery. The words 'every contract on a bill' mean the liability that one incurs by becoming a party to the bill in the capacity of drawer, indorser or acceptor—what this liability is in each case can be found under sections 54 and 55.

The delivery can be actual or constructive, i.e., it can be the actual physical transfer of the bill or it can be some act that shows immediate intention to deliver (in the case of acceptance, even mere advice of acceptance sent by the acceptor to the person entitled to the bill will suffice for delivery).

A man may sign a bill in the capacity as drawer, acceptor or indorser but with no intention of delivering the bill, or he may sign and then deliver it subject to the recipient's fulfilling a certain condition. In neither case will a valid delivery have occurred. In the latter case, if the recipient does not fulfil the condition his title will be defective by reason of non-delivery, since delivery will not be complete until the condition is fulfilled. (N.B.—Conditional *delivery* is quite a regular procedure whereas conditional *drawing* of the bill would invalidate it—see section 3.)

In the former case where no delivery at all is made, if a person takes a bill without authority he can have no title because of absence of delivery. But here again the law makes an exception in favour of a holder in due course. Should such a bill be negotiated to a holder in due course a complete and valid delivery by all prior parties will be *conclusively* presumed in his favour. For example, if Brown signs some bearer cheques and leaves them in his desk from which they are stolen. Brown, the drawer, will not be liable on the grounds of non-delivery. But if the thief negotiates the cheques to a holder in due course the latter can enforce payment, and it will avail Brown nothing to plead non-delivery since a valid delivery will be conclusively presumed in favour of the holder in due course.

But in view of section 20, the above applies only in the case of *complete* bills. If the bearer cheques had been left inchoate by Brown then a valid delivery would be presumed *only until the contrary were proved.* The onus of proof will be, of course, on the party trying to escape liability.

Even with a complete bill, as subsection 3 states, if it is *not* in the hands of a holder in due course, a valid delivery will be presumed only until the contrary is proved. Thus in the example, if the thief had *given* the bearer cheques to someone as a gift, the new holder, not being a holder in due course (see section 29), would probably fail to enforce payment since valid delivery by Brown would be presumed only until Brown proved non-delivery.

Capacity and Authority of Parties. [Sections 22–26]

22. Capacity of parties

(1) Capacity to incur liability as a party to a bill is co-extensive with capacity to contract.

Provided that nothing in this section shall enable a corporation to make itself liable as drawer, acceptor or indorser of a bill unless it is competent to it so to do under the law for the time being in force relating to corporations.

(2) Where a bill is drawn or indorsed by an infant, minor, or corporation having no capacity or power to incur liability on a bill, the drawing or indorsement entitles the holder to receive payment of the bill, and to enforce it against any other party thereto.

This section merely confirms that the Bills of Exchange Act is no exception to general law concerning the ability of persons to engage in a contract. It is well-known that, as a general rule, a minor cannot be sued for debt. That is why a bank would never in normal circumstances grant an unsecured loan to anyone under age.

Thus a person without power to contract, can sign a bill in any capacity, drawer, acceptor or indorser, and his signature will serve to transfer the bill. But if the bill is dishonoured, he cannot be sued, and the holder would have to rely upon his rights against the other parties.

23. Signature essential to liability

No person is liable as drawer, indorser, or acceptor of a bill who has not signed it as such: Provided that—

(1) Where a person signs a bill in a trade or assumed name, he is liable thereon as if he had signed it in his own name,

(2) The signature of the name of a firm is equivalent to the signature by the person so signing of the names of all persons liable as partners in that firm.

A 'firm' is a partnership, and the word should not be used in reference to a limited company. It is quite customary for a partner to

sign on behalf of the whole partnership by merely writing the name
of the partnership, e.g., 'Burt & Co'.

24. Forged or unauthorised signature

Subject to the provisions of this Act, where a signature on a
bill is forged or placed thereon without the authority of the
person whose signature it purports to be, the forged or
unauthorised signature is wholly inoperative, and no right to
retain the bill or to give a discharge therefor or to enforce
payment thereof against any party thereto can be acquired
through or under that signature, unless the party against
whom it is sought to retain or enforce payment of the bill is
precluded from setting up the forgery for want of authority.

Provided that nothing in this section shall affect the
ratification of an unauthorised signature not amounting to a
forgery.

This section should be studied in conjunction with sections 54 and
55.

Forgery   This is the act of falsely making or altering any document with the intention of defrauding or prejudicing another person. Thus, altering a cheque without authority from £8 to £80 is
a felony as much as is the forgery of the drawer's signature to a
cheque.

Forged signature   This requires no explanation. It should be
observed, however, that it is not essential that the signature should
resemble in character the genuine one, providing there is the
intention by the forger that the forged signature shall be accepted
as genuine and that someone shall suffer thereby.

Unauthorised signature   If Brown is the Director of a company he
will probably have the authority to sign on behalf of the company,
e.g., '*per pro* Blank Co Ltd, J Brown'. If Brown is the office boy,
however, it is most unlikely that he will be authorised to sign on
behalf of the company, and should he do so without authority, the
signature will be unauthorised. The Act makes no distinction
between a forged signature and an unauthorised one except that it

recognises the power in certain cases to ratify an unauthorised one. For example, if office-boy Brown indorsed bills payable to the company and sent them for collection on account of the company no harm would occur, and the company would no doubt ratify the unauthorised indorsements if subsequently they were discovered. But where an unauthorised signature is tantamount to forgery, ratification would be impossible. No-one can ratify a forgery as it would be compounding a felony.

This section states that the forged or unauthorised signature is wholly inoperative, i.e., *for the purpose of transfer of title* it is no signature at all, and the space it occupies can be treated as a blank piece of paper.

Forgery of the drawer's signature   If the drawer has not signed (and he cannot have signed if his signature has been forged), then the document without the drawer's signature cannot be a bill. Section 3 says that a bill is an unconditional order in writing *signed by the person giving it*. If it is not so signed it is not a bill at all. Consequently there can be no holder and no title to it—in fact, it is in itself, as far as it presumes to be a bill, worthless. As this section says, no-one can have any right to retain the 'bill', discharge or pay it, or force payment of it. So, if Robinson steals Brown's cheque book, forges Brown's signature to a cheque for £10 and gets Jones to cash it for him, Jones will be the victim of the fraud. He cannot sue Brown on the cheque since Brown did not sign it—his only remedy lies against Robinson (if he can be found) for what it is worth. If Jones presented the cheque to the bank on which it is drawn (the drawee bank) and obtained payment, the bank would be unable to debit Brown's account with it, for the bank's only authority for debiting the account is Brown's genuine signature; (the section itself says 'there is no right to give a discharge therefor'—i.e., the bank cannot pay it). The bank would lose the money unless (and this would be very rare) the forgery was immediately discovered after payment and Jones quickly advised of the discovery before he could alter his position on the strength of receiving payment. In such a rare case Jones presumably might have to refund. But if the bank had paid the forger Robinson, then its only right would be against the forger, for what it was worth.

Forgery of an essential indorsement   Where a bill is drawn payable to order, the payee must indorse it before he can negotiate it to someone else. Similarly where a bill has been negotiated and, by special indorsement, is made payable to order (of the indorsee), the indorsement of the indorsee is essential before he can negotiate it further. What is the position if that essential indorsement is forged? Let us take an example.

A bill for £1,000 payable to Surtees is drawn by Smith and issued to Surtees.

Surtees, by special indorsement negotiates it to Silverman.

Silverman by special indorsement negotiates it to Savage.

At this stage Savage loses the bill and the finder forges the signature of Savage to a special indorsement in favour of Snook to whom the finder negotiates the bill.

Snook by special indorsement negotiates it to Snail.

Snail by special indorsement negotiates it to Sinker.

At each stage of the negotiation of the bill £1,000 is given, of course. There are seven people concerned in the bill (besides the thief) in the order of Smith, Surtees, Silverman, Savage, Snook, Snail and Sinker. Whilst the bill remains with Sinker, he hears that Savage has lost the bill and that his indorsement of the bill is a forgery. What appears to be Savage's special indorsement, 'Pay J Snook or order, H Savage', is, according to this section, no signature at all—a blank on the bill in effect. This means that the indorsements on the reverse of the bill will be interpreted as follows:

(1) Pay J Silverman or order, B Surtees.
(2) Pay H Savage or order, J Silverman.
(3) Blank.
(4) Pay B Snail or order, J Snook.
(5) Pay M Sinker or order, B Snail.

The important point to observe is Snook's indorsement. It will be seen that Snook has no right to transfer the bill to Snail since it was not in effect payable to Snook when he had it—it was still payable to Savage and required Savage's indorsement to put the bill in a deliverable state. Since Snook had no power to transfer it, Snail has no right to the bill nor any power, likewise, to transfer it to Sinker, and Sinker remains with a bill to which he, similarly, has no title. He will be compelled to restore the bill to Savage when the latter demands it. Now, since the indorsements after the forgery are inoperative for the passage of title, the bill, in effect, remains as it was when Savage lost it, viz., still payable to him. Consequently, in effect, Sinker is a person in possession of an unindorsed order bill payable to Savage—in short, he has no title to the bill. Thus, we say that no title can be obtained through the forgery of an essential indorsement and no-one can be a *holder* (see section 2) where there is such a prior forgery.

Normally with a bill where no forgery has occurred, we can see the chain of special indorsements from the payee to the final holder. If a bill passes from Drawer A to Payee B and thence by special indorsements to C, D, E and finally to F, F is the holder. What is the position if the bill is dishonoured? Firstly, let us see in what way a bill can be dishonoured. All bills can be dishonoured by the drawee's failure to pay. In addition, bills payable at a certain future date can be dishonoured by the drawee's failure to accept the bill. Further, even if the drawee did accept the bill, he may fail to pay it when it matures. Thus dishonour of a bill may mean:

(1) Drawee's failing to accept;
(2) Drawee's failing to pay;
(3) Acceptor's failing to pay;
(In the third case, the acceptor can be sued on his signature).

When F finds his bill has been dishonoured, he has an immediate right of recourse agains E who must refund to F the equivalent of whatever F gave to him for the bill. Similarly E can demand repayment from D and D from C, C from B, and B from the drawer A. To save time, F could approach the drawer A for repayment and 'by pass' all the intermediary stages with the same result. In fact he can enforce payment from any of the prior parties, e.g., F could compel C to pay him and in this way two of the intermediary stages would be 'by-passed'.

Where this 'claiming back' can take place, there is a perfect title because the chain of title back to the drawer is perfect.

Pictorially it appears thus:

Drawer			*Holder*
A			F
Indorser	*Indorser*	*Indorser*	*Indorser*
B *(Payee)*	C	D	E

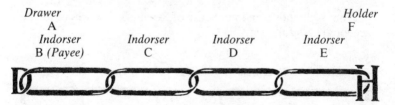

Every link holds good since the indorsement of each 'link' is genuine. You might say that F has a 'hold on the drawer' since the latter is 'chained' to him.

But in the case of Savage & Co, above, the chain would appear thus:

Sinker has no hold on the drawer or Surtees or Silverman; a link is missing that would otherwise have bound them to him. Thus a good title to a bill can be exemplified in *the right to sue the drawer* (and all the parties between).

Under section 55 we shall see what the position of Sinker is in such a case. We know that he has no title to the bill but it would not be fair that he should lose his money whilst Snook, the victim of the fraud, suffers nothing. We shall see how he can get his money back from Snail or Snook and how, if he obtains it from Snail, Snail can recover from Snook. Someone must lose by reason of the fraud and obviously, the person eventually must be Snook, the victim.

What happens to the chain of title when the bill is accepted? This can be best shown pictorially for though another party is added, it does not alter the original chain of title. The drawee, by accepting the bill, becomes primarily liable for payment, and the drawer and indorsers become sureties for him.

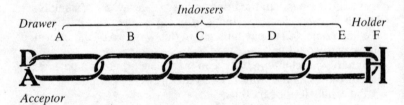

What is the position in the case of Savage & Co, where the bill is accepted? As follows:

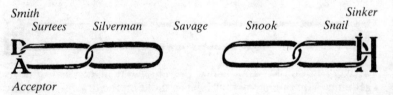

Sinker here has no rights against the acceptor since the chain does not connect them.

Forgery of payee's indorsement   The chain:

Drawer
 Payee   *Indorsers*

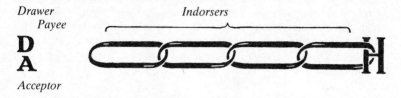

Acceptor

Again both drawer and acceptor are severed from the 'holder' and he has no rights against them.

Forgery of drawer's signature

Indorsers

 Payee

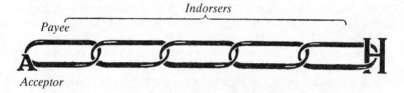

Acceptor

Though there is no drawer and, therefore, no valid bill, the acceptor remains tied to the 'holder' and is liable for payment as though there had been no forgery at all (see section 54). In addition, of course, each indorser is liable to the 'holder'.

Forgery of acceptance   We have seen that a good title to a bill is exemplified in the tight chain from drawer to holder and that in the chain the connection to the acceptor was incidental and not vital to the chain. Consequently, a forged acceptance does not interfere with the chain of title and merely means that the bill is unaccepted.

Exceptions   This section commences with the words 'Subject to the provisions of this Act'. The general rule is that you cannot retain, discharge or enforce payment of the bill where an essential signature is forged, but the exceptions, 'the provisions of this Act', are in sections 54 and 55 which may provide a 'money back guarantee' *but never a good title*. Further exceptions are in sections 60 and 80 where bankers are protected in their dealings with cheques bearing forged indorsements and these, like sections 54 and 55, will be reviewed in due course. Section 4 of the Cheques Act 1957 introduces another exception relating to bankers collecting cheques with forged indorsements. This exception was found originally in section 82 of the Act under review (now repealed). The only other exception is section 72(1) which decides that if a forgery was perpetrated in a foreign country where the law permits a holder to obtain a good title in spite of the forgery, then we shall recognise their law *as it applies to that signature* and treat it as genuine for the purpose of English law.

Forgery of indorsements on bearer bills   A bearer bill, as section 2 showed, is transferred by mere delivery and not indorsement and delivery. Therefore, whilst the bill is payable to bearer, all indorsements, as far as the title of the holder is concerned, can be ignored. If the bill is payable to bearer because it was originally drawn thus, no indorsement is essential for transfer, though such bills are often indorsed nevertheless. Consequently a forged indorsement will not affect the title of the holder. Similarly where an order bill is made payable to bearer by an indorsement in blank, no further indorsement is necessary whilst it remains payable to bearer. If it is nevertheless indorsed and a subsequent indorsement is found to be a forgery, the title of the holder will be unaffected. He remains in each case *the person in possession of a bill payable to bearer and is consequently the holder* (see section 2). In short, an indorsement to a bearer bill is not an *essential* indorsement. If it is genuine, then it simply makes the relative party liable on the bill in case of dishonour and it is *not* a means of transferring the bill—see section 58 for further amplification.

Payment of a bill bearing a forgery of an essential indorsement   If the acceptor pays a bill before a forged indorsement is discovered, he will be paying someone who has no title to the bill. The rightful owner in this case can force the acceptor to pay again. The acceptor, however, can recover from the person to whom he paid the money in the first instance. If that person refunds to the acceptor, then he can claim from his transferor – transferee can claim from his transferor until the victim of the fraud, as before, is left to stand the loss. The position is somewhat different in regard to cheques (see section 60).

Estoppel   It is true to say as a general rule that a man cannot be liable on a bill if he has not signed it even though a forged signature purporting to be his appears on the bill. But there is one exception. If a man knows that his signature to a bill has been forged and he, by his actions or by his silence, wittingly leads others to believe that such is his genuine signature, then the courts will not allow him later to plead that his signature was forged and escape liability thereby. In short he will be 'estopped from denying the signature to be his'. This rule appears quite fair—he cannot have it both ways! Suppose a man observes that his wife, whose handwriting is like his own has, at times, paid her housekeeping bills by cheques drawn on his account, signing her husband's name so similarly that the drawee bank has paid them. It is his obvious duty to stop the practice and advise the bank that although no harm has been done, they have in fact paid away his money against signatures that were not his. If he fails to do this, and later his wife draws his balance of £5,000 in the same way as before and deserts him, he will not be allowed to deny the signature. By his silence, he has led the bank to rely upon the wife's 'forgery' as being his genuine signature and he will lose the £5,000.

25. Procuration signatures
A signature by procuration operates as notice that the agent has but a limited authority to sign, and the principal is only bound by such signature if the agent in so signing was acting within the actual limits of his authority.

Where a person authorises another to sign for him as his agent, the agent's authority, except in very rare cases, will be limited. So, where a bill bears a '*per pro*' signature that signature is considered in itself as a warning to anyone taking the bill that the agent *may* have exceeded his authority. As this section states, the principal is not bound if the agent exceeds his authority.

Exceptions   (1) *Limited companies*   These must obviously act through agents. The general rule applies here, as before, that the company is not bound by the unauthorised acts of its agents, (e.g., its directors) *but* provided a person has examined the company's regulations (its memorandum and articles of association) and it *appears* that the agent is acting within his authority, then the company will be bound by that agent even though in fact he did exceed his authority. This ruling emerged from the celebrated case of *Royal British Bank v Turquand* and is now known as the rule in *Turquand's* case.

(2) *Paying banker*   Obviously a banker cannot initiate investigations into the circumstances behind the drawing of every cheque by agents for principals. Where an agent is authorised to draw cheques '*per pro*' his principal, a mandate is lodged with the paying banker. If the agent uses his authority to draw money for purposes not authorised by the principal, the bank will be protected by the mandate lodged.

> **Example**   A authorises his clerk B to draw cheques on A's account and lodges a mandate to that effect at his bankers. B draws cheques for payment of his own gambling debts and they are duly paid when presented. Although B had no authority for these transactions, the paying banker will still be able to debit A's account.

26.   Person signing as agent or in representative capacity
(1) Where a person signs a bill as drawer, indorser or acceptor, and adds words to his signature, indicating that he signs for or on behalf of a principal, or in a representative character, he is not personally liable thereon; but the mere addition to his signature of words describing him as an agent, or as filling a representative character, does not exempt him from personal liability.

(2) In determining whether a signature on a bill is that of the principal or that of the agent by whose hand it is written, the construction most favourable to the validity of the instrument shall be adopted.

This is self-explanatory and requires no amplification. Nevertheless, the case of *Durham Fancy Goods Ltd v Michael Jackson (Fancy Goods) Ltd etc.* ([1968] 2 All ER 987) is interesting since it exemplifies this subsection. Michael Jackson, a Director of the defendant company, accepted a bill on behalf of the company signing 'For and on behalf of M Jackson (Fancy Goods) Ltd M Jackson.'

He was unaware that his company's name had been incorrectly stated. The bill was dishonoured on maturity and the defendant company went into liquidation. The holders of the bill sued Mr Michael Jackson as personally liable on the bill under the Companies Act. Apart from the latter we can see that his liability would arise personally under this section since the company of which he had been a Director had ceased to exist. To hold that the signature was that of the agent personally was in fact 'a construction most favourable to the validity of the bill'. (In the event the judgment was based on other grounds that do not concern us here.)

The Consideration for a Bill. [Sections 27–30]

27. Value and holder for value

(1) Valuable consideration for a bill may be constituted by:
  (a) Any consideration sufficient to support a simple contract;
  (b) An antecedent debt or liability. Such a debt or liability is deemed valuable consideration whether the bill is payable on demand or at a future time.

(2) Where value has at any time been given for a bill the holder is deemed to be a holder for value as regards the acceptor and all parties to the bill who became parties prior to such time.

(3) Where the holder of a bill has a lien on it arising either from contract or by implication of law, he is deemed to be a holder for value to the extent of the sum for which he has a lien.

Value   Subsection (1) states what the Act will recognise as value given for a bill. It is broad and accepts any consideration (goods, services, money, etc.), that is 'sufficient to support a simple contract' or, in other words, sufficient to constitute a 'bargain' or a 'deal'. It is broader than common law since it recognises a past debt or liability as value (e.g., a ton of coal delivered on 1 May will be considered 'value' for my cheque that I hand to the coal merchant on 31 May). In our study of negotiable instruments we found that adequate value is not essential and that giving inadequate value will not upset a person's good title. A bill is no exception to this rule and giving inadequate value will not affect a person's title to a bill unless the inadequacy reflects lack of good faith (see p. 21 on 'Good faith').

Illegal considerations   For examples of these, the student is referred to more advanced works on bills of exchange. A discussion of what may constitute illegal consideration is considered to be outside the scope of this work. In passing, however, it may be said that whilst an illegal consideration will avoid a simple contract, such a consideration will not necessarily avoid it as against a transferee for value, without notice of the illegal consideration, in the case of a negotiable instrument.

Holder for value   Subsection (2) states that a holder for value is not only a holder who has himself given value for the bill but can also be any holder, whether he gave value or not, providing some previous holder gave value. But in each case whether he gives value or not, he must be a *holder* (see section 2).

> **Example**   A draws a cheque for £100 payable to B, his tailor, for a suit. B specially indorses the cheque to C for wages owing to him. C, in turn specially indorses it to his wife D and hands it to her as a birthday present. D specially indorses it to E and gives it to him for a wedding present. Although E, the ultimate holder, gave no value for the cheque he is nevertheless a holder for value since prior parties, viz., B and C gave value in their turn for the cheque. Similarly, whilst the cheque was in her possession, D, too, was a holder for value although she gave no value for it herself. If, when E presents it for payment, the cheque is dishonoured, what is E's position? In normal circumstances, every prior party would be liable to E but in this case the position is somewhat different. Since he did not give value for the cheque he cannot sue D, obviously. (After all, if a man gave you a pound note as a gift and you subsequently discovered it was a counterfeit note you could not take legal action to compel him to replace the counterfeit by a genuine note.) Similarly, E cannot sue C on the dishonoured cheque for C also received no value when he transferred the cheque. But E can sue A, the drawer, and/or B, the payee, for both received value for the cheque. They are 'parties to the bill who became parties prior to such time that value was given'.

N.B.—(1) Where the bill has been accepted the acceptor is liable to a holder for value in any case, whether the latter gave value or not.

(2) If in the above example, E had negotiated the cheque to F and F had taken the bill in accordance with the requirements of section 29, F would have been a holder in due course and, as such, would have had the right to enforce payment against *all* prior parties including D and C, since he is completely unaffected by the absence of consideration between prior parties.

The case of *Diamond v Graham* ([1968] WLR 1061) gave us a practical application of subsection 2. Here, a Mr Diamond had given his own cheque for £1,650 to a Mr Herman in consideration of that person's delivering a cheque to Diamond drawn by Graham for a like amount'. Herman was then to issue his cheque to Graham for a similar amount somewhat later so that Herman got temporary financial assistance. Thus three cheques were drawn: (1) Graham's cheque in favour of Diamond, (2) Diamond's cheque in favour of Herman (the real borrower) and (3) Herman's cheque in favour of Graham. In the event only one cheque, that drawn by Diamond, was paid on presentation and he was the loser in a somewhat complicated transaction. Diamond held Graham's cheque which had been dishonoured. That cheque had been obtained by Herman from Graham and Herman had given consideration for the cheque, namely, his own cheque in favour of Graham. Thus Diamond held a cheque for which someone had previously given value and the Court of Appeal held that subsection 2 of this section applied in favour of Diamond who therefore could enforce payment against Graham.

Lien   Subsection (3). This is the right of a creditor to retain property of his debtor until such time as the debt is discharged. The extent of the lien is measured by the amount of the debt. If you borrow £500 from a bank depositing security valued at £1,000, the bank secures lien on that security to the extent of £500. Should the security be a bill of exchange then the bank becomes a holder for value of the bill to the extent of the lien.

[Although there was no question of lien, we nevertheless should examine the case of *Barclays Bank Ltd v Aschaffenburger Zellstoffwerke AG* (1967), recalling the old case of *Thornton v Maynard* ((1875) LR 10 CP 695) which dealt with the position of a holder of a bill who holds it partly for himself and partly as trustee for another. The law is that the party liable to pay the bill may, if such be the case, raise against the trustee any defence or counterclaim which he has against the person behind the transaction, that is the beneficiary of that part of the bill for whom the trustee holds it. It is not a question now of a holder being a holder for value to the extent of his lien since in this case Barclays Bank had bought under discount certain bills from Black-Clawson International Ltd, giving 73.161% of the face value (and obviously holding the bills as trustee for Black-Clawsons to the extent of 26.839%). The case simply shows that it is possible to be a holder for value as to part of a bill and a mere holder as to the remainder of the bill. As to 73.161%, the bank had a perfect title free from equities but as to the 26.839%

the bank's rights were subject to any set-off or counterclaim that the acceptors of the bills had against the beneficial owners of the 26.839%.]

This section should be studied along with section 29 and the difference between a holder for value and a holder in due course observed. Briefly, the latter is a certain type of holder for value who has an unassailable title even though his transferor had a defective one or one subject to any other equity. A holder for value who happens not to be a holder in due course, however, cannot have any better title than his transferor had.

28. Accommodation bill or party

(1) An accommodation party to a bill is a person who has signed a bill as drawer, acceptor or indorser, without receiving value therefor, and for the purpose of lending his name to some other person.

(2) An accommodation party is liable on the bill to a holder for value; and it is immaterial whether, when such holder took the bill, he knew such party to be an accommodation party or not.

Here is the only exception to section 27 regarding holder for value. We saw that C and D in the example in section 27 were not liable to E if the cheque was dishonoured since they did not receive value. But C and D could not be classified as accommodation parties since they did *not* sign the bill with the express purpose of lending their names to someone. If they had signed with that intention they *would* have been liable to E. What, then, is an accommodation party? An example will illustrate.

Suppose A being pressed for money, arranges with his wealthy friend B that A shall draw a 3 months bill on B and that B shall accept the bill. B, in accepting, becomes liable for payment in 3 months' time although A has given him no value. As the party primarily liable for payment is the wealthy B the bill is first-class security and A can raise money on it (i.e., 'discount' it) immediately. A hopes that, in three months' time when B will be called on to pay, his financial stringency will have disappeared and that he will be able to provide B with funds to pay the bill. B has signed the bill as acceptor to oblige or accommodate A. Consequently B is an accommodation party. This method of obtaining funds employed by A is sometimes known as 'kite flying' or 'raising the wind'.

One more example. Suppose that you are spending a few days at the home of a friend and that you run short of money. You cannot, we presume, cash a cheque at a local bank since they have no knowledge of you or any guarantee that your cheque would be paid by the drawee bank. (We will have to forget about bankers' cards for this purpose.) But your friend can introduce you to his bankers and indorse your cheque with his own signature making himself liable on it in the event of dishonour. Now, your friend's bankers will doubtlessly oblige you and cash you the cheque (i.e., buy it from you and become a holder for value) since they know that, in the event of dishonour, their own customer, being liable as an indorser, must re-imburse them (i.e., they will be able to debit his account). Your friend has lent his name to oblige you; he has received no value for undertaking liability on the cheque and is, by consequence, an accommodation party.

It is essential to observe that an accommodation party is not liable to the party accommodated since the latter gives him no value for undertaking the liability. Thus, if A accommodates B by accepting his bill and B negotiates the bill to C, C can enforce payment against A and B. If A refuses to pay the bill at maturity, C may sue A immediately or obtain the money from B. If he chooses the latter course, B must pay the bill which is discharged by his payment. He has no right to sue the acceptor as a drawer always has with normal dishonoured bills.

Finally, do not conclude that every bill which bears the signature of an accommodation party is an 'accommodation bill'. The latter term should be used only to describe a bill where the accommodation party is the acceptor (as in the first example). The reason for this can be found in section 59(3) which states that an accommodation bill is discharged on payment by the party accommodated. A moment's thought will show that this must be the case only where the acceptor is the accommodation party. If any other party, say an indorser, was the accommodation party, then, if the party accommodated paid the bill the latter, though unable to sue the accommodation party, could nevertheless sue the acceptor and the bill would not be discharged whilst the acceptor remained liable on it.

Example   *Accommodation bill*   X accepts for the accommodation of A, the drawer. X is the accommodation party and A, the party accommodated. B is the payee, C an indorsee and D the eventual holder. If X, the acceptor, refuses to pay the bill at maturity, then A, the drawer, is next in order of liability. If D compels A to pay then the bill is discharged since X is not liable to A as he merely obliged him by accepting the bill. Thus the bill is discharged by payment by the party accommodated.

Not an accommodation bill although bearing the signature of an accommodation party   A is the drawer, X is the acceptor and B, the payee. B asks C, a wealthy man, to indorse the bill so that he can easily discount the bill at Bank D. If X, the acceptor fails to pay, the Bank D can force payment from any prior party including B, the party accommodated. If it compels B to pay, then the bill is not discharged by his payment since B would still have the right to sue the acceptor for payment.

(Whilst on this subject, sections 46(2) and 50(2) should be observed.)

29. Holder in due course

(1) A holder in due course is a holder who has taken a bill, complete and regular on the face of it, under the following conditions; namely:

   (a) That he became the holder of it before it was overdue, and without notice that it had been previously dishonoured, if such was the fact;

   (b) That he took the bill in good faith and for value, and that at the time the bill was negotiated to him he had no notice of any defect in the title of the person who negotiated it.

(2) In particular the title of a person who negotiates a bill is defective within the meaning of this Act when he obtained the bill, or the acceptance thereof, by fraud, duress, or force and fear, or other unlawful means, or an illegal consideration, or when he negotiates it in breach of faith, or under such circumstances as amount to a fraud.

(3) A holder (whether for value or not), who derives his title to a bill through a holder in due course, and who is not himself a party to any fraud or illegality affecting it, has all the rights of that holder in due course as regards the acceptor and all parties to the bill prior to that holder.

The definition of a holder in due course is given in subsection (1) here, and almost every word is important. Let us analyse the definition.

'A holder in due course *is a holder.*'

We saw under section 24 that where a signature that is an essential link in the chain of title is forged, the chain is broken and no-one taking the bill after that forgery can be a 'holder'. Therefore, when the Act says that a holder in due course must be a holder it is obvious that no-one can be a holder in due course after forgery of an essential signature.

'Bill, *complete* and *regular* on the face of it.'

If the bill is not complete, then no-one who takes it can be a holder in due course. Thus, a person who takes an inchoate instrument, even though he may have authority to complete it, cannot be a holder in due course. (But note that acceptance is not necessary to make a bill complete.)

If the bill is not regular on the face of it then again no-one can be a holder in due course. For example, a bill marked 'Not Negotiable' or 'Not Transferable' is not regular on the face of it although quite valid.

'Before it was overdue.'

If a bill is due and payable on 21 September then on and after 22 September it is overdue and anyone taking the bill then cannot be a holder in due course though he may be a holder for value. Does this concern the holder of a *cheque*? Yes. Section 36(3) states that any bill payable on demand (including cheques) is deemed to be overdue when it appears on the face of it to have been in circulation for an unreasonable length of time. What is an unreasonable length of time will be judged by the facts of each case.

'Without notice that it had previously been dishonoured if such was the fact.'

One might observe here that this proviso seems unnecessary since if it had been dishonoured it would be overdue. This, however, is not always true. For example if a bill is drawn on 1 May payable 3 months after date it is due on 1 August. Yet a holder might present it for acceptance on 15 May and find acceptance refused by the drawee. This would be *dishonour of the bill by non-acceptance*, yet the bill would still be current and *not* overdue. A person taking such a bill with the knowledge that it has already been dishonoured in this way cannot be a holder in due course.

When a cheque is dishonoured by the drawee bank it will bear on the face of it the 'answer' or reason for non-payment such as 'Refer to Drawer', 'words and figures differ' etc. Thereafter any transferee of the cheque would patently have notice of previous dishonour.

'In good faith and for value.'

This has already been discussed under negotiable instruments and applies equally here (see pp. 20 and 21).

'Without notice of any defect in the title of his transferor.'

This proviso is intended to cover the whole field of equities besides the defect in title. A man who takes a bill knowing that his transferor's title is defective or subject to any equity, cannot claim to be free from those equities, i.e., he cannot be a holder in due course. The same applies to all negotiable instruments.

'Notice' may be either particular or general; particular notice being knowledge of a particular fact avoiding the bill, and general or implied notice being knowledge of some illegality or fraud but lacking precise details. In addition, wilful or fraudulent refusal to investigate the circumstances surrounding the bill when such circumstances obviously invite investigation may be deemed to be general or implied notice.

If a holder can fulfil *all* the requirements of this definition, he is a holder in due course and certain of a complete and unassailable title to the bill. He will be the true owner and vested with all the rights that can accrue to a holder of a negotiable instrument, particularly the right to be free from all prior defects in title and equities affecting prior holders. (His rights are fully set out in section 38.) The title of any other holder, whether he be a holder for value (section 27) or merely a holder (section 2), can be defeated by prior equities and defects (though if there be no prior equity, etc., the title of a holder or a holder for value will be quite good).

Example A draws a bearer cheque and hands it to B in payment of goods received. C steals it from B and hands it to D as a gift. D subsequently gets E to 'cash' it for him, E fulfilling all the requirements of section 29. Now, when C stole the cheque he became the holder (section 2—the bearer of a bearer bill is the holder of it) although B was the true owner. When D received it as a gift, though innocent of the theft, he was not a holder in due course since he did not give value himself, though since value had at one time been given (i.e., by B) he was a holder for value (section 27). But a holder for value who is not a holder in due course is not free from prior defects in title. Consequently, though D was a holder for value, he was subject to B's right of restoration, an equity, and B remained the true owner. But when E gave value for it to D, he became the holder in due course, i.e., not only the holder but the true owner (and B ceased to be the true owner there and then). Thus, though there can be at one and the same time a holder and a separate true owner, there cannot be a *holder in due course* and a separate true owner since a holder in due course is *always* the true owner and there cannot be more than one owner of a bill at the same time.

If, in this example, E gives the cheque to his wife as a gift, his wife cannot be a holder in due course since she does not give value—she will be merely a holder for value. But providing she has not been implicated in C's theft of the bill, she will have all the rights of a holder in due course that her husband had because she derived her title through a holder in due course. This is outlined in subsection (3) of this section.

N.B.—The payee of a bill cannot be a holder in due course since a bill (as this section says) is *negotiated* to a holder in due course, whereas a bill is always issued to the payee.

Before leaving this subject, it should be made quite clear that a person need not necessarily fulfil all the requirements of section 29 to get a good title to a bill. Where there has been no prior irregularity, defect in title or equity, then the holder of a bill will doubtless be the true owner. It is only where absence of title, defects in title or equities have existed that section 29 becomes important, since only by complying with it can a holder be free from the defects in title of prior parties and be, in fact, the true owner.

30. Presumption of value and good faith

(1) Every party whose signature appears on a bill is *prima facie* deemed to have become a party thereto for value.

(2) Every holder of a bill is *prima facie* deemed to be a holder in due course; but if in an action on a bill it is admitted or proved that the acceptance, issue, or subsequent negotiation of the bill is affected with fraud, duress, or force and fear, or illegality, the burden of proof is shifted, unless and until the holder proves that, subsequent to the alleged fraud or illegality, value has in good faith been given for the bill.

Value is always presumed to have been passed between parties and good faith is always presumed until the contrary is proved.

For example, subsection (2) says quite clearly that where the title of a possessor of a bill is in dispute, then the onus of proof that the possessor cannot comply with all the requirements of section 29 is on the person who challenges the possessor. In other words 'possession is nine points of the law', an old saying that is very broadly reflective of the English law of property. If I have a bill, the law presumes it is mine absolutely (that I am the holder in due course) until someone proves something to the contrary to upset my title.

Subsection (2) also makes clear what we learn in section 29(3), viz. that a holder who derives his title through a holder in due course and who is not a party to any fraud etc. affecting it is possessed of all the rights of a holder in due course. The fact that such a holder had knowledge of previous fraud will not alter his position either, providing he had not been a party to it.

Negotiation of Bills. [Sections 31–38]

31. Negotiation of a bill

(1) A bill is negotiated when it is transferred from one person to another in such a manner as to constitute the transferee the holder of the bill.

(2) A bill payable to bearer is negotiated by delivery.

(3) A bill payable to order is negotiated by the indorsement of the holder completed by delivery.

(4) Where the holder of a bill payable to his order transfers it for value without indorsing it, the transfer gives the transferee such title as the transferor had in the bill, and the transferee in addition acquires the right to have the indorsement of the transferor.

(5) Where any person is under obligation to indorse a bill in a representative capacity, he may indorse the bill in such terms as to negative personal liability.

This section illustrates that a bill conforms with instruments known as negotiable, i.e., transferable by delivery where payable to bearer and transferable by indorsement and delivery where payable to order. Note how subsection (4) agrees with 'Deliverable state' (see p. 22).

32. Requisites of a valid indorsement

An indorsement in order to operate as a negotiation must comply with the following conditions, namely:

(1) It must be written on the bill itself and be signed by the

indorser. The simple signature of the indorser on the bill, without additional words, is sufficient.

An indorsement written on an allonge, or on a 'copy' of a bill issued or negotiated in a country where 'copies' are recognised, is deemed to be written on the bill itself.

(2) It must be an indorsement of the entire bill. A partial indorsement, that is to say, an indorsement which purports to transfer to the indorsee a part only of the amount payable, or which purports to transfer the bill to two or more indorsees severally, does not operate as a negotiation of the bill.

(3) Where a bill is payable to the order of two or more payees or indorsees who are not partners all must indorse, unless the one indorsing has authority to indorse for the others.

(4) Where, in a bill payable to order, the payee or indorsee is wrongly designated, or his name is mis-spelt, he may indorse the bill as therein described, adding, if he think fit, his proper signature.

(5) Where there are two or more indorsements on a bill, each indorsement is deemed to have been made in the order in which it appears on the bill, until the contrary is proved.

(6) An indorsement may be made in blank or special. It may also contain terms making it restrictive.

Sections 32 to 35 are the only sections dealing with correctness of indorsements, etc., and today one is guided largely by custom and legal decision. The importance of indorsements to bankers has diminished very considerably by the passing of the Cheques Act 1957. See later.

A bill payable to bearer requires no indorsement since it is transferable by mere delivery and anyone indorsing it does so voluntarily, taking on himself the liability of an indorser as set out in section 55. A bill payable to order must be indorsed by the holder before he transfers it. His indorsement is a token of his intention to transfer it and his willingness to accept the liability of section 55. In addition, the holder who presents the bill for payment should indorse it in blank before he receives payment from the drawee or acceptor unless the bill be a cheque presented to the drawee Bank through the agency of a collecting Bank in which case indorsement is unnecessary (Cheques Act 1957).

Allonge   It is quite conceivable that the back of a much-transferred bill can become full with indorsements. In such a case, a slip of paper is gummed to the bill as a continuation sheet for indorsements and is called an 'allonge'. The last indorsement on the actual bill should be made partly on the bill and partly on the allonge. (French *allonger* means 'to make longer'.)

Subsection (2)   An indorsement can be made to transfer part of the bill. This is quite legal but the indorsement will not operate as a negotiation of the bill. A person taking a bill in such circumstances would have no title to the bill, though he may use the bill as evidence of the contract made between himself and his transferor. Compare this with someone who holds a bill as security and is a holder for value to the extent of his lien (section 27 (3)).

On the whole, section 32 is fairly straightforward.

33. Conditional indorsement
Where a bill purports to be indorsed conditionally the condition may be disregarded by the payer, and payment to the indorsee is valid whether the condition has been fulfilled or not.

Under section 21 it was observed that conditional delivery was not a valid delivery until the condition was fulfilled but that a holder in due course could ignore the condition that concerned, not him, but prior parties to him. In a similar manner the drawee or acceptor, on paying the bill, can ignore any conditional indorsement (which is merely conditional delivery), and if he pays the holder, the bill is discharged although the condition may not have been fulfilled.

34. Indorsement in blank and special indorsement
(1) An indorsement in blank specifies no indorsee, and a bill so indorsed becomes payable to bearer.

(2) A special indorsement specifies the person to whom, or to whose order, the bill is to be payable.

(3) The provisions of this Act relating to a payee apply with the necessary modifications to an indorsee under a special indorsement.

(4) When a bill has been indorsed in blank, any holder may convert the blank indorsement into a special indorsement by writing above the indorser's signature a direction to pay the bill to or to the order of himself or some other person.

Here is the authority for what was given as an amplification of section 2 concerning 'holder' and 'bearer'. It should be observed what an indorsement in blank is and how it differs from a special indorsement. An indorsement in blank is the mere signature of the indorsee and, on an order bill, converts the bill to one payable to bearer. But any holder can convert an indorsement in blank into a special indorsement and re-convert the bill into an order bill as it was originally drawn. This section is clear as to procedure.

35. Restrictive indorsement

(1) An indorsement is restrictive which prohibits the further negotiation of the bill or which expresses that it is a mere authority to deal with the bill as thereby directed and not a transfer of the ownership thereof, as, for example, if a bill be endorsed 'Pay D only', or 'Pay D for the account of X', or 'Pay D or order for collection'.

(2) A restrictive indorsement gives the indorsee the right to receive payment of the bill and to sue any party thereto that his indorser could have sued, but gives him no power to transfer his rights as indorsee unless it expressly authorises him to do so.

(3) Where a restrictive indorsement authorises further transfer, all subsequent indorsees take the bill with the same rights and subject to the same liabilities as the first indorsee under the restrictive indorsement.

Subsection (1) means, briefly, that if a bill is restrictively indorsed, prohibiting further transfer, it becomes in effect not transferable and therefore, not negotiable. Now, since the bill becomes not negotiable as soon as it is restrictively indorsed, the indorsee receives an instrument that is not a negotiable instrument but a non-transferable document of title. His title will depend entirely on that of his transferor, and, should the latter have no title or one subject to equities then his title will suffer likewise.

Subsections (2) and (3) clearly indicate what the indorsee's rights are. These rights cannot be transferred unless authority to do so is expressed in the bill. This additional authority will not revive the negotiability but it will revive the transferability. Consequently future holders will be subject to any equity that may have affected any holder who took the bill subsequent to the restrictive indorsement.

For examples of correct and incorrect indorsements, the student is referred to 'Questions on Banking Practice' of the Institute of Bankers and text books on practical banking.

36. Negotiations of overdue or dishonoured bill

(1) Where a bill is negotiable in its origin it continues to be negotiable until it has been (a) restrictively indorsed or (b) discharged by payment or otherwise.

(2) Where an overdue bill is negotiated, it can only be negotiated subject to any defect of title affecting it at its maturity, and thenceforward no person who takes it can acquire or give a better title than that which the person from whom he took it had.

(3) A bill payable on demand is deemed to be overdue within the meaning and for the purposes of this section, when it appears on the face of it to have been in circulation for an unreasonable length of time. What is an unreasonable length of time for this purpose is a question of fact.

(4) Except where an indorsement bears date after the maturity of the bill, every negotiation is *prima facie* deemed to have been effected before the bill was overdue.

(5) Where a bill which is not overdue has been dishonoured any person who takes it with notice of the dishonour takes it subject to any defect of title attaching thereto at the time of dishonour, but nothing in this subsection shall affect the rights of a holder in due course.

As was seen in section 8, a bill may be issued in such a way as to negative its negotiability (e.g., a bill drawn payable to AB *only*, or one marked 'Not Transferable' or 'Not Negotiable'). But if a bill is issued in the normal way, full negotiable, then only a restrictive indorsement, its becoming overdue, or actual discharge of the bill can subsequently negative the negotiability. (What the discharge of a bill is we shall see under sections 59 to 64.)

Subsection (2) includes an example of the use of the word 'negotiate' when the writer strictly meant 'transfer for value' (see p. 24, 'Use of word "Negotiable"'). Under section 29 we observed that no-one can become a holder in due course of an overdue bill since a holder in due course must take the bill *before it is overdue*. From the study of sections 27 and 29 we found that only a holder in due course of a bill can obtain all the rights attaching to a holder of a negotiable instrument. Since a person taking an overdue bill cannot be a holder in due course, he is merely a holder or, at best, a holder for value. Consequently, as we observed under section 27, he must be affected by any prior equitable interest, etc.

Subsection (3) (which does not apply to promissory notes) particularly concerns cheques, since a cheque is a bill of exchange payable on demand and drawn on a banker (section 73). A person taking a cheque cannot in every case be quite certain that it is not overdue since each case is judged on its merits. But the onus of proof that the cheque *is* overdue is on the person trying to avoid liability on it. But an overdue cheque is not necessarily a stale cheque. The latter is generally one bearing a date six months or more prior to the date of presentation for payment and the drawee banker to whom the cheque is presented will return it marked 'stale cheque' or 'out of date', preferring not to pay it until it can be confirmed by the drawer. In some cases a cheque that has been in circulation over six months, may still be considered not overdue by the courts, whereas in other cases a period of circulation of less than 12 days may be considered by them as sufficient to make a cheque overdue.

Subsection (4) Very few indorsements on a bill are ever dated, but if one should be then it will be relatively easy to determine whether it was made before the bill became due. Where no date is included, an indorsement is presumed to have been made before the bill became due for payment. If some party to the bill, in his desire to escape liability on it, pleads that a certain indorsement was made after the due date of the bill (or in other words, after the maturity of the bill), the onus of proof is on him.

Subsection (5) merely repeats what we learnt from section 29. Anyone taking a dishonoured bill which is *not* overdue (e.g., a bill dishonoured by non-acceptance) is still affected by any previous equities, etc., but if he can show that he did not know of the dishonour, he may be able to establish himself as a holder in due course and consequently be free from previous equities.

37. Negotiation of bill to party already liable thereon
Where a bill is negotiated back to the drawer, or to a prior indorser or to the acceptor, such party may, subject to the provisions of this Act, re-issue and further negotiate the bill, but he is not entitled to enforce payment of the bill against any intervening party to whom he was previously liable.

> **Example**   A bill for £100 is drawn by A payable to B and is accepted by X. B negotiates it to C, C to D, D to E and E to F. F who owes B £100 hands him the bill in payment. B, the original payee can still negotiate the bill further to (say) G. If he does, the order of liability of the parties will be:
>
> 1. X, 2. B, 3. C, 4. D, 5. E, 6. F, 7. B, 8, G
>
> If the bill is dishonoured by X then G can sue him or enforce payment from any other party. If he compels B (his transferor) to pay him, B *cannot* enforce payment from C, D, E or F obviously since they could in their turn enforce it from B in his earlier capacity as payee.

38. Rights of the holder
The rights and powers of the holder of a bill are as follows:
   (1) He may sue on the bill in his own name.
   (2) Where he is a holder in due course he holds the bill free from any defect of title of prior parties, as well as from mere personal defences available to prior parties among themselves, and may enforce payment against all parties liable on the bill.
   (3) Where his title is defective (a) if he negotiates the bill to a holder in due course, that holder obtains a good and

complete title to the bill, and (b) if he obtains payment of the bill the person who pays him in due course gets a valid discharge for the bill.

This is partly a repetition of section 29. We have already found that a holder in due course obtains a title free from any prior equities.

Observe that providing payment is made to the holder the bill will be discharged even though the holder may not be a holder in due course. This relieves the acceptor or drawee of the duty of ascertaining whether the holder is in fact the true owner. This is repeated in section 59 which says that a valid discharge of the bill can be the 'payment in due course of the bill by the acceptor or drawee' and that 'payment in due course' is 'payment made at or after the maturity of the bill to the HOLDER thereof'.

It matters nothing if any party liable on the bill possesses any counterclaim against the holder. Such counterclaim cannot be exercised so as to delay or avoid payment of the bill to a holder enforcing payment thereof. In *Ceroba SNC v SIP (Industrial Products) Ltd* ([1976] 1 Lloyds Rep 271) the acceptor refused payment to the holder on the grounds of a counterclaim against him. Held that a counterclaim must be a separate action. 'Pay up on the bill first and pursue claims later' is the doctrine.

General Duties of the Holder. [Sections 39–52]

The following sections deal with the *duties* of a holder, since a holder must fulfil certain obligations imposed by the Act in order to preserve his rights allowed him in section 38.

39. When presentment for acceptance is necessary
(1) Where a bill is payable after sight, presentment for acceptance is necessary in order to fix the maturity of the instrument.

(2) Where a bill expressly stipulates that it shall be presented for acceptance, or where a bill is drawn payable elsewhere than at the residence or place of business of the drawee, it must be presented for acceptance before it can be presented for payment.

(3) In no other case is presentment for acceptance necessary in order to render liable any party to the bill.

(4) Where the holder of a bill drawn payable elsewhere than at the place of business or residence of the drawee, has not time, with the exercise of reasonable diligence, to present the bill for acceptance before presenting it for payment on the day that it falls due, the delay caused by presenting the bill for acceptance before presenting it for payment is excused, and does not discharge the drawer and indorsers.

Obviously the necessity for presentment for acceptance does not concern bills payable on demand, at sight, or on presentation. Consequently, sections 39 and 44 concerning acceptance will not apply to such bills (including cheques).

It should be clearly understood that, except as provided by subsection (2) here, a holder of a bill payable after *date* is under no obligation to present the bill for acceptance. Such a step, however, is recommended since, if the drawee does accept, he becomes liable for payment, and by consequence, the bill is more desirable and more likely to be paid at maturity by virtue of the acceptor's liability.

But where a bill is drawn payable after sight, presentment for acceptance is essential, since, until the date of sighting by the drawee is ascertained it will be impossible to calculate the maturity date of the bill. The sooner a bill is 'sighted' the sooner it will be due for payment. If a bill is drawn on 1 January payable 30 days after sight then, until it is sighted no-one can decide the date the drawee should pay. If it is presented for acceptance on 13 January then the 30 days commence to run from then making the due date 12 February. (It should be remembered, however, that the time runs from the date of sighting *only if the bill is accepted*. Otherwise, as section 14(3) stated the time runs from the date the bill is noted or protested for non-acceptance (see section 51).)

Bills that have been accepted by the drawee are thereafter called 'acceptances' as well as 'bills'.

40. Time for presenting bill payable after sight

(1) Subject to the provisions of this Act, when a bill payable after sight is negotiated, the holder must either present it for acceptance or negotiate it within a reasonable time.

(2) If he does not do so, the drawer and all indorsers prior to that holder are discharged.

(3) In determining what is a reasonable time within the meaning of this section, regard shall be had to the nature of the bill, the usage of trade with respect to similar bills, and the facts of the particular case.

Here simply is the warning to the holder of an unaccepted bill payable after sight that, unless he presents it for acceptance or negotiates it, both within a reasonable length of time, he will lose his right of recourse against the drawer and all indorsers (a right which he will want if the bill is dishonoured). Subsection (3) clearly states what is considered a reasonable length of time.

N.B.—The law does not say that it is illegal to delay the presentation for acceptance but provides for the interests of prior parties already liable on the bill. It would not be fair to them if it were possible to retain their liability indefinitely by delaying the presentation. Every person who becomes a party to a bill undertakes to pay the bill should the drawee fail to do so. It is, therefore, inequitable that a subsequent holder should be able to extend that liability as long as he chooses after a reasonable time has elapsed. The parties liable have every right to know that the period of their liability shall be as short as is reasonably possible.

41. Rules as to presentment for acceptance, and excuses for non-presentment

(1) A bill is duly presented for acceptance which is presented in accordance with the following rules:

(a) The presentment must be made by or on behalf of the holder to the drawee or to some person authorised to accept or refuse acceptance on his behalf at a reasonable hour on a business day and before the bill is overdue.

(b) Where a bill is addressed to two or more drawees, who are not partners, presentment must be made to them all, unless one has authority to accept for all, then presentment may be made to him only.

(c) Where the drawee is dead presentment may be made to his personal representative.

(d) Where the drawee is bankrupt, presentment may be made to him or to his trustee.

(e) Where authorised by agreement or usage, a presentment through the post office is sufficient.

(2) Presentment in accordance with these rules is excused,
and a bill may be treated as dishonoured by non-acceptance:

(a) Where the drawee is dead or bankrupt, or is a fictitious person or a person not having capacity to contract by bill.

(b) Where, after the exercise of reasonable diligence,
such presentment cannot be effected.

(c) Where, although the presentment has been irregular,
acceptance has been refused on some other ground.

(3) The fact that the holder has reasons to believe that the
bill, on presentment, will be dishonoured does not excuse
presentment.

This requires no amplification.

42. Non-acceptance

When a bill is duly presented for acceptance and is not
accepted within the customary time, the person presenting it
must treat it as dishonoured by non-acceptance. If he does
not, the holder shall lose his right of recourse against the
drawer and indorsers.

Like section 40, this section is concerned with the interests of prior
parties liable on a bill. They have a right to know as soon as possible whether the drawee has accepted it, or whether by reason of
non-acceptance, they may be called upon to pay the bill. The customary time mentioned here is 24 hours and no extension is
allowed to the drawee. If the acceptance is not forthcoming within
24 hours the bill must be treated as dishonoured by non-
acceptance and the usual notice given to all prior parties.

43. Dishonour by non-acceptance and its consequences

(1) A bill is dishonoured by non-acceptance:

(a) when it is duly presented for acceptance, and such an

acceptance as is prescribed by this Act is refused or
cannot be obtained; or
(b) when presentment for acceptance is excused and the
bill is not accepted.

(2) Subject to the provisions of this Act when a bill is dishonoured by non-acceptance, an immediate right of
recourse against the drawer and indorsers accrues to the holder, and no presentment for payment is necessary.

Observe the three ways in which a bill is dishonoured by non-
acceptance.
(1) Where acceptance is refused;
(2) Where acceptance cannot be obtained (e.g., where the drawee
cannot be found or where he deliberately avoids the presentment);
(3) Where acceptance is excused, as provided by section 41(2).

The main point of this section is that as soon as a bill is dishonoured by non-acceptance, the holder's right of recourse against
prior parties arises immediately without his having to present it for
payment later. The amount he can recover is dealt with under section 57.

44. Duties as to qualified acceptance

(1) The holder of a bill may refuse to take a qualified acceptance, and if he does not obtain an unqualified acceptance
may treat the bill as dishonoured by non-acceptance.

(2) Where a qualified acceptance is taken, and the drawer
or an indorser has not expressly or impliedly authorised the
holder to take a qualified acceptance, or does not subsequently assent thereto, such drawer or indorser is discharged
from his liability on the bill.

The provisions of this subsection do not apply to a partial
acceptance, whereof due notice has been given. Where a
foreign bill has been accepted as to part, it must be protested
as to the balance.

(3) When the drawer or indorser of a bill receives notice
of a qualified acceptance, and does not within a reasonable
time express his dissent to the holder he shall be deemed to
have assented thereto.

Section 19 stated what a qualified acceptance is. The holder is not obliged to take such an acceptance, however, if a general acceptance is refused. He can simply treat the bill as dishonoured by non-acceptance and take action accordingly. In fact, he is advised to take nothing but a general acceptance unless he has obtained the consent of all parties liable on the bill. If he did take a qualified acceptance without their consent then any or all of the prior parties may relieve themselves of their liability by refusing consent.

Exception   If partial acceptance is offered (e.g., where the drawee offers to accept to the extent of £800 a bill drawn for £1,000), then there is no harm in taking it since it makes the drawee liable for part of the amount of the bill and this is better than nothing. But the holder would still treat the bill as dishonoured by non-acceptance as to the balance and advise all prior parties of the qualified acceptance. In addition, if the bill was a foreign one he would protest it for the unaccepted balance (see section 51).

45. Rules as to presentment for payment
Subject to the provisions of this Act a bill must be duly presented for payment. If it be not so presented the drawer and indorsers shall be discharged.

A bill is duly presented for payment which is presented in accordance with the following rules:

(1) Where the bill is not payable on demand, presentment must be made on the day it falls due.

(2) Where the bill is payable on demand, then, subject to the provisions of this Act, presentment must be made within a reasonable time after its issue in order to render the drawer liable, and within a reasonable time after its indorsement, in order to render the indorser liable.

In determining what is a reasonable time, regard shall be had to the nature of the bill, the usage of trade with regard to similar bills, and the facts of the particular case.

(3) Presentment must be made by the holder or by some person authorised to receive payment on his behalf at a reasonable hour on a business day, at the proper place as hereinafter defined, either to the person designated by the bill as payer, or to some person authorised to pay or refuse

payment on his behalf if with the exercise of reasonable diligence such person can there be found.

(4) A bill is presented at the proper place:

(a) Where a place of payment is specified in the bill and the bill is there presented.

(b) Where no place of payment is specified, but the address of the drawee or acceptor is given in the bill, and the bill is there presented.

(c) Where no place of payment is specified and no address given, and the bill is presented at the drawee's or acceptor's place of business if known, and, if not, at his ordinary residence if known.

(d) In any other case if presented to the drawee or acceptor wherever he can be found, or if presented at his last known place of business or residence.

(5) Where a bill is presented at the proper place, and after the exercise of reasonable diligence no person authorised to pay or refuse payment can be found there, no further presentment to the drawee or acceptor is required.

(6) Where a bill is drawn upon, or accepted by two or more persons who are not partners, and no place of payment is specified, presentment must be made to them all.

(7) Where the drawee or acceptor of a bill is dead, and no place of payment is specified, presentment must be made to a personal representative, if such there be, and with the exercise of reasonable diligence he can be found.

(8) Where authorised by agreement or usage a presentment through the Post Office is sufficient.

This long section looks frightening at first glance but closer analysis will show that the rules are very reasonable and quite clearly stated. Briefly, the section means that a bill must be presented for payment to the drawee or his agent on the due date at the proper place at a reasonable time on a business day and that failure in any of these respects will discharge the prior parties from liability.

Example   A Newcastle bank is asked by a customer to collect an accepted bill payable in Nottingham and they send it for collection to their branch in Mottingham in error. The delay in redirecting the bill to Nottingham results in the presentation for payment being made after the due date. If the acceptor pays the bill then no harm is occasioned by the delay, but if he dishonours it the customer will have lost his right of recourse against the prior parties (and the bank incidentally will very probably have to make good any loss that the customer may suffer by reason of the bank's delay).

46. Excuses for delay or non-presentment for payment

(1) Delay in making presentment for payment is excused when the delay is caused by circumstances beyond the control of the holder, and not imputable to his default, misconduct, or negligence. When the cause of delay ceases to operate presentment must be made with reasonable diligence.

(2) Presentment for payment is dispensed with:

(a) Where, after the exercise of reasonable diligence presentment, as required by this Act, cannot be effected.

The fact that the holder has reason to believe that the bill will, on presentment, be dishonoured, does not dispense with the necessity for presentment.

(b) Where the drawee is a fictitious person.

(c) As regards the drawer where the drawee or acceptor is not bound as between himself and the drawer, to accept or pay the bill, and the drawer has no reason to believe that the bill would be paid if presented.

(d) As regards an indorser, where the bill was accepted or made for the accommodation of that indorser, and he has no reason to expect that the bill would be paid if presented.

(e) By waiver of presentment, express or implied.

Apart from subsections (2)(c) and (2)(d) which concern bills bearing the signature of an accommodation party, this section is straightforward.

Subsection (2)(c)   If the drawee or acceptor is under no obligation, as far as the drawer is concerned, to pay the bill (where the bill has been accepted for the accommodation of the drawer), then presentment for payment is not necessary *in order to retain the liability of the drawer* as is the case with normal bills. But although failure to present for payment would not deprive the holder of his right of recourse against the drawer, it would still discharge the indorsers. So, to retain the liability of the other parties to the bill, presentment for payment should be made on the due date.

Subsection (2)(d)   If an indorser is the party who has been accommodated then, as before, failure to present the bill for payment would not discharge him from liability. But as it would discharge the drawer and the other indorsers (if any), it would be foolish not to present the bill on the due date.

Of course, in normal circumstances, every bill is presented for payment on the due date with the primary desire of obtaining payment. Incidental to this is the knowledge that, should payment not be obtained, the fact that presentment for payment was made on the due date retains for the holder the right of recourse to all prior parties.

Lastly, it should be remembered that if an acceptance is not presented for payment on the due date and the liability of prior parties is lost, the holder's position is not entirely hopeless. Firstly, the acceptor may pay the bill when it is eventually presented. Again, even if the acceptor refused to pay, the holder can still sue him on his acceptance by action at law any time during the next 6 years. Unfortunately, if for any reason such an action did not succeed or if the acceptor was found to be bankrupt, loss would be inevitable as the holder would be unable to turn to other parties for recourse.

47. Dishonour by non-payment
(1) A bill is dishonoured by non-payment (a) when it is duly presented for payment and payment is refused or cannot be obtained, or (b) when presentment is excused and the bill is overdue and unpaid.

(2) Subject to the provisions of this Act, when a bill is dishonoured by non-payment, an immediate right of recourse against the drawer and indorsers accrues to the holder.

This is similar to section 43 except that it concerns dishonour by non-payment as compared with dishonour by non-acceptance. The same right of recourse (section 57) against prior parties arises.

If the drawee or acceptor offers to pay the bill with a cheque instead of cash, the bill should not be surrendered until the cheque is cleared. The reason for this is that to surrender the bill would be tantamount to accepting the cheque in complete discharge of the bill. If the cheque was subsequently dishonoured by the drawee bank then the holder would have merely the right to sue the drawer of the dishonoured cheque, the right of recourse to the parties of the bill being lost as soon as the bill was surrendered.

Part payment   If part only of the amount of the bill is offered by the drawee or acceptor, the holder can take it or refuse it as he wishes. If he refuses it, he should take the normal proceedings on dishonour, but if he takes it he should indorse on the bill, a receipt for the amount of the part payment, retain the bill and treat it as dishonoured as to the balance. (Compare Partial Acceptance —section 44.) As a bird in the hand is worth two in the bush, it would seem that a holder would be well advised to take part payment and sue if necessary for the dishonoured balance against any party liable on the bill.

48. Notice of dishonour and effect of non-notice

Subject to the provisions of this Act, when a bill has been dishonoured by non-acceptance or by non-payment, notice of dishonour must be given to the drawer and each indorser, and any drawer or indorser to whom such notice is not given is discharged: Provided that—

(1) Where a bill is dishonoured by non-acceptance, and notice of dishonour is not given, the rights of a holder in due course, subsequent to the ommission, shall not be prejudiced by the omission.

(2) Where a bill is dishonoured by non-acceptance, and due notice of dishonour is given, it shall not be necessary to give notice of a subsequent dishonour by non-payment unless the bill shall in the meantime have been accepted.

We have seen that where a bill is dishonoured by non-acceptance or non-payment there is an immediate right of recourse against the parties liable on the bill. But this right of the holder to 'get back his money' exists only providing he gives notice of dishonour to the prior parties. What is a valid notice will be studied in the next section. There is no prescribed form of notice however, and any advice will do providing the words are sufficient to identify the bill and clearly state that the bill has been dishonoured by the drawee or acceptor.

Subsection (1) reminds us of section 29 which defined a holder in due course as a holder who takes a bill . . . without notice of previous dishonour if such has occurred. Thus, a bill may have been dishonoured by non-acceptance without notice of dishonour having been given to the prior parties. All the prior parties are discharged from liability *to the holder who* failed to give notice. But the bill is still capable of negotiation, the dishonour being one of non-acceptance, and if that holder negotiated it to a person who fulfilled all the requirements of section 29, the latter would be a holder in due course and the liability on the bill of prior parties would be revived.

Subsection (2) is quite straightforward.

49. Rules as to notice of dishonour

Notice of dishonour in order to be valid and effectual must be given in accordance with the following rules:

(1) The notice must be given by or on behalf of the holder, or by or on behalf of an indorser who, at the time of giving it, is himself liable on the bill.

(2) Notice of dishonour may be given by an agent either in his own name, or in the name of any party entitled to give notice whether the party be his principal or not.

(3) Where the notice is given by or on behalf of the holder, it enures for the benefit of all subsequent holders and all prior indorsers who have a right of recourse against the party to whom it is given.

(4) Where notice is given by or on behalf of an indorser entitled to give notice as hereinbefore provided, it enures for the benefit of the holder and all indorsers subsequent to the party to whom notice is given.

(5) The notice may be given in writing or by personal communication, and may be given in any terms which sufficiently identify the bill, and intimate that the bill has been dishonoured by non-acceptance or non-payment.

(6) The return of a dishonoured bill to the drawer or an indorser is, in point of form, deemed a sufficient notice of dishonour.

(7) A written notice need not be signed, and an insufficient written notice may be supplemented and validated by verbal communication. A misdescription of the bill shall not vitiate the notice unless the party to whom the notice is given is in fact misled thereby.

(8) Where notice of dishonour is required to be given to any person, it may be given either to the party himself, or to his agent in that behalf.

(9) Where the drawer or indorser is dead, and the party giving notice knows it, the notice must be given to a personal representative if such there be, and with the exercise of reasonable diligence he can be found.

(10) Where the drawer or indorser is bankrupt, notice may be given either to the party himself or to the trustee.

(11) Where there are two or more drawers or indorsers who are not partners, notice must be given to each of them, unless one of them has authority to receive such notice for the others.

(12) The notice may be given as soon as the bill is dishonoured and must be given within a reasonable time thereafter.

In the absence of special circumstances notice is not deemed to have been given within a reasonable time, unless:

(a) Where the person giving and the person to receive notice reside in the same place, the notice is given or sent off in time to reach the latter on the day after the dishonour of the bill.

(b) Where the person giving and the person to receive notice reside in different places, the notice is sent off on the day after the dishonour of the bill, if there be a post at a convenient hour on that day, and if there be no such post on that day then by the next post thereafter.

(13) Where a bill when dishonoured is in the hands of an agent, he may either himself give notice to the parties liable on the bill, or he may give notice to his principal. If he give notice to his principal, he must do so within the same time as if he were the holder, and the principal upon receipt of such

notice has himself the same time for giving notice as if the agent had been an independent holder.

(14) Where a party to a bill receives due notice of dishonour, he has after the receipt of such notice the same period of time for giving notice to antecedent parties that the holder has after the dishonour.

(15) Where a notice of dishonour is duly addressed and posted, the sender is deemed to have given due notice of dishonour, notwithstanding any miscarriage by the Post Office.

To ensure that every prior party to a bill remains liable to him, the holder should advise every party when dishonour occurs. But it is equally effective if the holder gives notice to only his own transferor providing that notice is passed down through indorsers until the payee notifies the drawer, e.g.:

DRAWER	PAYEE	INDORSERS	HOLDER	ACCEPTOR
A	B	C. D. E. F. G.	H	X

Where X dishonours the bill when presented to him by H the holder, H, to be certain of preserving the liability of all the indorsers and the drawer, should send them all individual notices. But if he merely advises G, then providing G gives notice to F, F to E, E to D, D to C, C to B, and B to drawer A, the same result is achieved. In practice the latter is the method generally adopted since it is fairly certain that prior parties will pass on the notice. Any party failing to do so would remain liable to the holder but lose his own right of recourse against the drawer and all who indorsed the bill before him. Nevertheless the slight risk attaching to this method is patent, and a holder to be absolutely safe should give notice of dishonour to all prior parties.

Subsection (3) should be noted. From this we see that if holder H in the previous example gives notice to payee B, that notice would retain B's liability not only to H but also to intervening parties, C, D, E, F and G. This, however, does not avoid giving notice to the latter parties if H wishes to retain their liability. A similar position arises (subsection (4)) for example where E gives notice to B. The latter then is liable to *all* parties subsequent to him including the holder and not merely C, D and E. Subsection (3) also provides for anyone taking the bill after dishonour and avoids the necessity for each new holder to advise prior parties of the dishonour of which they are already cognisant.

Notice of dishonour must be given within a reasonable time. The latter is *not* decided by the facts of each case here but is laid down clearly, viz., by the next day if the person to whom the notice is addressed lives in the same town or *posted* by the next day if he lives elsewhere.

Subsection (13) affects bankers particularly, since they often act as agents for customers in obtaining acceptances and collecting bills. Failure of the bank to advise in time may mean that the holder (the bank's customer) being ignorant of dishonour, fails to pass on the notice and loses the right of recourse against prior parties. If the holder suffers financially through this, the bank will have to recoup him. (This can occur in just the same way with cheques, e.g., where a cheque is returned unpaid to a collecting bank marked 'post-dated' and after re-presentation by the collecting banker who observes that by the time the cheque is presented through the clearing house it will be 'within date', it is again returned, this time through want of funds.) Banks, like all other agents, are allowed the same time as actual parties in which to advise their principals of dishonour.

Subsection (14), similarly, allows the same time to prior parties to pass on the notice of dishonour.

50. Excuses for non-notice and delay

(1) Delay in giving notice of dishonour is excused where the delay is caused by circumstances beyond the control of the party giving notice, and not imputable to his default, misconduct, or negligence. When the cause of delay ceases to operate the notice must be given with reasonable diligence.

(2) Notice of dishonour is dispensed with:

(a) When, after the exercise of reasonable diligence, notice as required by this Act cannot be given to or does not reach the drawer or indorser sought to be charged.

(b) By waiver express or implied. Notice of dishonour may be waived before the time of giving notice has arrived, or after the omission to give due notice.

(c) As regards the drawer in the following cases, namely, (1) where drawer and drawee are the same person, (2) where the drawee is a fictitious person or a person not having capacity to contract, (3) where the drawer is the person to whom the bill is presented for payment, (4) where the drawee or acceptor is as between himself and the drawer under no obligation to accept or pay the bill, (5) where the drawer has countermanded payment.

(d) As regards the indorser in the following cases, namely, (1) where the drawee is a fictitious person or a person not having capacity to contract, and the indorser was aware of the fact at the time he indorsed the bill, (2) where the indorser is the person to whom the bill is presented for payment, (3) where the bill was accepted or made for his accommodation.

This is fairly straightforward but the reader should observe:

Subsection (2)(b)   Under section 16(2) we saw that a party to the bill can waive as regards himself some of the holder's duties. Thus, if he drew or indorsed the bill adding the words 'notice of dishonour waived', then the holder need not advise him of dishonour if it occurred. In addition, observe that not only can it be waived by a party before the bill is dishonoured, but afterwards if, for example, the holder has omitted to notify him.

Subsection (2)(c)   Observe that a holder need not advise the drawer of dishonour:

(a) Where the drawer is also the drawee who has refused to accept or pay: (e.g., a banker's draft drawn by a branch bank on its head office).

(b) Where the drawee is a fictitous person or has no contractual powers. A fictitious person, obviously, cannot accept or pay a bill. Consequently, a bill drawn on such a drawee is bound to be dishonoured. The drawer knows this when he draws the bill and, therefore, notice of dishonour is wasted on him. Again, whether a person with no contractual powers accepts the bill or not, it means nothing to the holder since, even if the acceptance is given, it cannot be enforced in a court of law. Consequently, a person who draws on such drawees cannot expect to be advised of dishonour.

(c) Where the bill is presented to the drawer for payment. For example, a cheque is drawn by A on bank B payable to C. If the bank goes into liquidation before the cheque is presented the drawer must pay the cheque himself. In such circumstances, C would present the cheque to A for payment.

(d) Where the drawee (or acceptor) is under no obligation to the drawer to accept or pay the bill. For example; if A draws a cheque on bank B payable to C and A's account has insufficient funds to meet the cheque, the bank (the drawee) is under no obligation to pay the cheque. If it returns the cheque for lack of funds then C need not advise the drawer of the dishonour.

(e) Where the drawer has countermanded payment—obviously he will not require advice of something he has already done.

51. Noting or protest of bill

(1) Where an inland bill has been dishonoured it may, if the holder think fit, be noted for non-acceptance or non-payment, as the case may be; but it shall not be necessary to note or protest any such bill in order to preserve the recourse against the drawer or indorser.

(2) Where a foreign bill, appearing on the face of it to be such, has been dishonoured by non-acceptance it must be duly protested for non-acceptance, and where such a bill, which has not been previously dishonoured by non-acceptance, is dishonoured by non-payment it must be duly protested for non-payment. If it be not so protested the drawer and indorsers are discharged. Where a bill does not appear on the face of it to be a foreign bill, protest thereof in case of dishonour is unnecessary.

(3) A bill which has been protested for non-acceptance may be subsequently protested for non-payment.

(4) Subject to the provisions of this Act, when a bill is noted or protested, *it must be noted on the day of its dishonour* [it may be noted on the day of its dishonour and must be noted not later than the next succeeding business day]. When a bill has been duly noted, the protest may be subsequently extended as of the date of the noting.

(5) Where the acceptor of a bill becomes bankrupt or insolvent or suspends payment before it matures, the holder

may cause the bill to be protested for better security against the drawer and indorsers.

(6) A bill must be protested at the place where it is dishonoured: Provided that:

(a) When a bill is presented through the Post Office, and returned by post dishonoured, it may be protested at the place to which it is returned and on the day of its return if received during business hours, and if not received during business hours, then not later than the next business day.

(b) When a bill drawn payable at the place of business or residence of some person other than the drawee has been dishonoured by non-acceptance, it must be protested for non-payment at the place where it is expressed to be payable, and no further presentment for payment to, or demand on, the drawee is necessary.

(7) A protest must contain a copy of the bill, and must be signed by the notary making it, and must specify:

(a) The person at whose request the bill is protested.

(b) The place and date of protest, the cause or reason for protesting the bill, the demand made, and the answer given, if any, or the fact that the drawee or acceptor could not be found.

(8) Where a bill is lost or destroyed, or is wrongly detained from the person entitled to hold it, protest may be made on a copy or written particulars thereof.

(9) Protest is dispensed with by any circumstance which would dispense with notice of dishonour. Delay in noting or protesting is excused when the delay is caused by circumstances beyond the control of the holder, and not imputable to his default, misconduct, or negligence. When the cause of delay ceases to operate the bill must be noted or protested with reasonable diligence.

Subsection (4) The words in italics in this subsection were repealed and replaced by the words in square brackets by the Bills of Exchange (Time of Noting) Act 1917, section 1.

Where a bill is dishonoured, notice of dishonour must always be given to prior parties to retain their liability. In the case of foreign bills, however (see section 4) more than notice of dishonour is needed—the bill must also be protested by the holder. How is this done? The holder hands the bill to a notary public who again presents the bill for acceptance or payment as the case may be so as to obtain legal proof of dishonour. If the acceptance or payment is still unobtainable, the notary public draws up a protest, i.e., an official certificate evidencing the dishonour and stating why the protest is made, the demand made to the drawee (or acceptor) and the answer he gave. On the reverse of the certificate is a copy of the bill. The certificate is signed by the Notary.

This form of protest is recognised the world over and international law demands it as legal proof of dishonour. Failure to obtain the protest would mean that all parties (excluding the acceptor of course) would be released from their liability.

Are there any circumstances when even an inland bill can be protested? In two cases only.

(1) Before *any* bill is accepted for honour or paid for honour it must be protested (see section 65–68).

(2) Where the acceptor becomes bankrupt or insolvent before the bill matures then, although a protest is not essential it may be advisable 'for better security'. How does 'better security' arise from this? It does not mean that the holder can demand actual security from the previous parties (though in some countries, incidentally, he can). The only effect in this country is that the bill can then be accepted for honour as though actual dishonour by non-acceptance had, in fact, taken place.

A protest must be made by the day following the day of dishonour. This is very little grace especially when the holder is not quite certain that a protest is actually necessary in the circumstances. Consequently, the law provides for a procedure called 'Noting'. This is again done by a notary public who re-presents the bill and if the acceptance or payment is still refused, he attaches a slip of paper to the bill showing the answer he received, the date, his charges and his initials. This is much cheaper than the formal protest. But its main purpose is to extend the time in which a protest can be made (section 93).

Apart from this, the only other occasion when noting serves any purpose is on the dishonour of a bill by non-acceptance where the bill is payable after sight. Section 14(3) provides that the maturity of such a bill is calculated from the date of noting or protest for non-acceptance. In such circumstances the holder of an inland bill would note it in order to obtain the maturity date and without any intention of subsequently protesting it.

For Householder's Protest, see section 94.

A notary public is a solicitor with special powers. Not every solicitor is a notary public.

52. Duties of holder as regards drawee or acceptor

(1) When a bill is accepted generally presentment for payment is not necessary in order to render the acceptor liable.

(2) When by the terms of a qualified acceptance presentment for payment is required, the acceptor, in the absence of an express stipulation to that effect, is not discharged by the omission to present the bill for payment on the day that it matures.

(3) In order to render the acceptor of a bill liable it is not necessary to protest it, or that notice of dishonour should be given to him.

(4) Where the holder of a bill presents it for payment, he shall exhibit the bill to the person from whom he demands payment, and when a bill is paid the holder shall forthwith deliver it up to the party paying it.

This is straightforward.

Liabilities of Parties. [Sections 53–58]

53. Funds in hands of drawee

(1) A bill, of itself, does not operate as an assignment of funds in the hands of the drawee available for the payment thereof, and the drawee of a bill who does not accept as required by this Act is not liable on the instrument. This subsection shall not extend to Scotland.

(2) In Scotland, where the drawee of a bill has in his hands funds available for the payment thereof, the bill operates as an assignment of the sum for which it is drawn in favour of the holder, from the time when the bill is presented to the drawee.

Assignment of funds   If I have money deposited in a bank or held by someone on my behalf I can transfer some or all of it by using a negotiable instrument (bill of exchange) or a deed of assignment. The difference between the two in England (as far as this section is concerned) is:

Bill of exchange   The person holding my money is under no obligation to pay the money as I direct unless he accepts the bill (which he does voluntarily—there is no legal compulsion).

Assignment   Once the assignment or notice thereof is presented to the person holding the funds he must, whether he desires it or not, hold the money in trust for the assignee—he is legally bound to act on my assignment. (Compare Negotiability and Assignability, p. 18).

In Scotland, on the other hand, a bill does operate as an assignment of funds. This has an important effect on banking. If a person presents to a bank in Scotland a cheque drawn on that branch and the cheque cannot be paid there and then because of some irregularity or lack of funds to cover it, the bank must take details of the cheque and reserve sufficient funds (or the whole of the credit balance if less) to provide for the cheque on its second presentation.

In England no such provision is made since the bill is not recognised as an assignment. This conforms with the established rule that between a drawee bank and the holder of a cheque drawn thereon, there is no privity of contract (i.e., the bank has no *duty* whatever to the holder of the cheque—its duty is to its customer, the drawer, although it may be *liable* to the true owner (not necessarily the holder) of a cheque should it pay the cheque to someone other than the true owner—see sections 60 and 80).

54. Liability of acceptor
The acceptor of a bill, by accepting it:

(1) Engages that he will pay it according to the tenor of his acceptance.

(2) Is precluded from denying to a holder in due course:

(a) The existence of the drawer, the genuineness of his signature, and his capacity and authority to draw the bill;

(b) In the case of a bill payable to drawer's order, the

then capacity of the drawer to indorse, but not the genuineness of validity of his indorsement;

(c) In the case of a bill payable to the order of a third person, the existence of the payee and his then capacity to indorse, but not the genuineness or validity of his indorsement.

Subsection (2) is important here and is known as 'the estoppel of the acceptor'. Take the following extract: 'The acceptor . . . is precluded from denying to a holder in due course the existence of the drawer, the genuineness of his signature and his capacity and authority to draw the bill'. This means that the acceptor cannot refuse payment to a holder in due course on the excuse that—

(a) the drawer does not exist; or
(b) the drawer's signature is a forgery; or
(c) the drawer had no capacity or authority to draw the bill (e.g., where Brown, the office boy, draws a bill for his firm signing on behalf of the firm).

What is the effect of this? Under section 24 we saw how to ascertain whether a person in possession of a bill was a holder or not; whether he had any title to the bill or not. We saw that forgery or an essential signature (drawer's or indorser's) broke the chain of title and that the person in possession of the bill had NO title to it whatever. Section 54, however, affords some recourse to the person in possession of a 'bill' where the drawer's signature is forged. The forgery, of course, means that the document is not a valid bill and that consequently there can be no title to it as a bill. But section 54 says that an acceptor cannot plead this as an objection to paying the bill—in fact he is responsible for the genuineness of the drawer's signature and, in effect, guarantees that it is genuine. So, the possessor knows that, although he has no title to a 'bill' where the drawer's signature is forged, he will have the right to insist that the acceptor pays, i.e., he will have the *rights* of a holder in due course against the acceptor (though he is certainly *not* a holder in due course). It is considered that the words 'holder in due course' in subsection (2) here, are intended to mean 'someone who, except for the forgery of the drawer's signature, etc., would have been a holder in due course'.

The acceptor, however, is not responsible for the genuineness of indorsements. Where an essential indorsement is forged we know that the possessor of the bill has no title. In addition, then, he cannot even hold the acceptor liable as he can when the drawer's signature is forged. This was explained pictorially under section 24.

55. Liability of drawer or indorser
(1) The drawer of a bill by drawing it:
  (a) Engages that on due presentment it shall be accepted and paid according to its tenor, and that if it be dishonoured he will compensate the holder or any indorser who is compelled to pay it, provided that the requisite proceedings on dishonour be duly taken;
  (b) Is precluded from denying to a holder in due course the existence of the payee and his then capacity to indorse.
(2) The indorser of a bill by indorsing it:
  (a) Engages that on due presentment it shall be accepted and paid according to its tenor, and that if it be dishonoured he will compensate the holder or a subsequent indorser who is compelled to pay it, provided that the requisite proceedings on dishonour be duly taken;
  (b) Is precluded from denying to a holder in due course the genuineness and regularity in all respects of the drawer's signature and all previous indorsements;
  (c) Is precluded from denying to his immediate or a subsequent indorsee that the bill was at the time of his indorsement a valid and subsisting bill, and that he had then a good title thereto.

The drawer is responsible for payment should the bill be dishonoured by the drawee (or acceptor). Before the bill is accepted he is primarily liable for payment; after acceptance, the acceptor takes on the primary liability and the drawer becomes second in the order of liability or, in other words, becomes surety for the acceptor. If the drawer is called upon by a holder in due course to pay the bill, he cannot escape liability merely because the payee does not exist or has no capacity to indorse.

The indorser is responsible to all who became parties subsequent to himself and also to the holder. He agrees to pay the bill, should the drawee (or acceptor) dishonour it. Further, his indorsement acts as a guarantee to any subsequent holder in due course that all the indorsements prior to his own are genuine. All this means—

(1) that where the drawer's signature is forged the possessor of the 'bill' has the rights of a holder in due course against all indorsers (besides against the acceptor through section 54);

(2) that in the case of a forged indorsement the possessor of the bill has the rights of a holder in due course (though no actual title to the bill) against all parties who indorsed subsequent to the forgery (but, of course, no rights against the acceptor—section 54).

An example will make this clear.

A draws a bill payable to B. B transfers it to C by special indorsement. The bill is stolen from C by Z. Z forges C's signature to a special indorsement and transfers the bill to D. By further special indorsements the bill passes to E and thence to F. Under section 24, F has no title to the bill since he is not a holder, the bill being still payable to C. A and B will not recognise anyone else but C as having any right to the bill. C, in his turn, can compel F to restore the bill to him or pay him its equivalent. F, consequently, would be in a very poor position but for this section which says that those who indorsed the bill after the forgery (D and E) guarantee the genuineness of all indorsements prior to their own (which includes the forgery purporting to be C's indorsement). In this case they cannot escape their liability that they undertake in subsection (2)(a). Thus F can recover from E and E from D. D the victim of the forgery will bear the loss unless he can recover from Z, the forger.

Resumé of sections 54 *and* 55
The sections do NOT enable a good title to be obtained through a forgery. They merely grant the *rights* of a holder in due course against certain parties (i.e., the right to recover money paid for the bill). They do not concern parties who signed prior to the forgery (except in the unusual case where an acceptor signs before the drawer)—they merely concern parties who sign *subsequent* to the forgery, and decide who among those parties will be the one to bear the loss caused by the forgery.

56. Stranger signing bill liable as indorser
Where a person signs a bill otherwise than as drawer or

acceptor, he thereby incurs the liabilities of an indorser to a holder in due course.

This section provides for the person who indorses a bill without receiving value for assuming the liability. Strictly the signature is not an indorsement, but the point is purely academic since he assumes the liability of an indorser. (See section 28.)

57. Measure of damages against parties to dishonoured bill

Where a bill is dishonoured, the measure of damages, which shall be deemed to be liquidated damages, shall be as follows:

(1) The holder may recover from any party liable on the bill, and the drawer who has been compelled to pay the bill may recover from the acceptor, and an indorser who has been compelled to pay the bill may recover from the acceptor or from the drawer, or from a prior indorser:

(a) The amount of the bill;

(b) Interest thereon from the time of presentment for payment if the bill is payable on demand, and from the maturity of the bill in any other case;

(c) The expenses of noting, or, when protest is necessary, and the protest has been extended, the expenses of protest.

(2) In the case of a bill which has been dishonoured abroad, in lieu of the above damages, the holder may recover from the drawer or an indorser, and the drawer or an indorser who has been compelled to pay the bill may recover from any party liable to him, the amount of the re-exchange with interest thereon until the time of payment.

(3) Where by this Act interest may be recovered as damages, such interest may, if justice require it, be withheld wholly or in part, and where a bill is expressed to be payable with interest at a given rate, interest as damages may or may not be given at the same rate as interest proper.

Order of liability

(a) *Before acceptance*

   (1) Drawer, (2) Payee (or first indorser), (3) second indorser (4) third indorser, etc.

(b) *After acceptance*
      (1) Acceptor, (2) Drawer, (3) Payee (or first indorser), (4)
            second indorser, etc.

In (a) if the holder cannot secure the acceptance or payment, the party primarily liable to pay is the drawer.

In (b) if the acceptor refuses payment, he is *still* primarily liable for payment and can be sued by the holder, if the latter so desires. The holder, however, will most likely seek to recover the amount of the bill from the drawer or other party rather than incur the expense and delay of a suit against the acceptor.

In both cases where the bill is dishonoured the holder can recover from any prior party the whole amount of the bill. The prior parties are, in effect, guarantors since they make themselves liable for payment if the holder fails to obtain acceptance or payment from the drawee (or acceptor). But each party is individually liable for the whole amount, NOT pro-rata with the other parties. The holder, if he chooses, can recover from the drawer or he may prefer to obtain it from an indorser, If the holder recovers from an indorser, the latter can in his turn recover from any indorser prior to himself or the drawer. Ultimately the drawer must pay if the drawee or acceptor fails to do so.

What can be recovered besides the full amount of the bill? Subsection (1) is very precise and clear on this point.

Subsection (2) covers bills drawn in foreign currency.

Example   A bill drawn for 12,000 French francs is sold by X to a bank for £1,000 (rate, £1 = 12 fr). The bill is subsequently dishonoured and the bank requires X to repay them. The sum he pays may not be £1,000 as before. If, for example, the rate has in the meantime moved to 11.8, the bank will require £1016.90 plus expenses of protest, etc.

58. Transferor by delivery and transferee
(1) Where the holder of a bill payable to bearer negotiates it by delivery without indorsing it, he is called a 'transferor by delivery'.

(2) A transferor by delivery is not liable on the instrument.

(3) A transferor by delivery who negotiates a bill thereby warrants to his immediate transferee being a holder of value that the bill is what it purports to be, that he has a right to transfer it, and that at the time of transfer he is not aware of any fact which renders it valueless.

Observe that a transferor by delivery is the holder of a *bearer* bill who transfers it without indorsement. A holder of a bill payable to *order* who transfers it without indorsing it is NOT a transferor by delivery, and section 31(4) applies to him.

The reader may wonder why the Act says 'without indorsement' since a bearer bill is transferable by mere delivery. The answer is found in section 56 which states that anyone placing his signature to a bill (other than as drawer or acceptor) incurs the liability of an indorser. This obtains even if the indorsement (as in the case of bearer bills) is not essential. It is quite usual for a transferee of a bearer bill to insist on the transferor's indorsement before he consents to take it, so that if the bill is unpaid the transferor will be liable *on the bill* as an indorser.

Section 58, however, provides that where the transferor of a bearer bill does not indorse, he is *not* liable *on the bill*. But his freedom from liability is not complete for this section provides that, where the transferee gave value to the transferor by delivery, the latter is liable to recoup his transferee (and him only) if—

(a) the bill is a forgery (i.e., not what it purports to be); or
(b) the transferor by delivery knows at the time of transfer that the bill will not be paid (aware of any fact that renders it valueless); or
(c) the transferor by delivery has a defective title (as the Act says 'has no right to transfer it').

Example 1   A draws a cheque payable to B or order and issues it to B. B indorses it in blank and negotiates it to C. C, without further indorsement, negotiates it to D. When D presents it for payment he finds that payment has been stopped. Can D recover from C? C is a transferor by delivery and is not liable on the bill. He is liable to his immediate transferee for value (D) if at the time he negotiated it, he knew payment was stopped, otherwise he is free from liability.

Example 2   C receives a bearer cheque from one of his customers. He negotiates it to D without indorsement. When D presents it for payment, the cheque is returned 'signature differs' and it is subsequently found that the drawer's signature has been forged. C is a transferor by delivery. As he warrants to his immediate transferee for value that the bill is 'what it purports to be' he will be liable to D since the cheque being a forgery is obviously not what it purports to be.

Observe that section 58 covers *all* bearer bills, not only those drawn originally to bearer but also order bills indorsed in blank.

A similar situation arises where a party actually signs a bill but adds *sans recours*, 'without recourse'. He avoids liability *on the bill*, but, like a transferor by delivery, he is still liable to his immediate transferee for value in any of the three cases given above.

Discharge of Bill. [Sections 59–64]

59. Payment in due course

(1) A bill is discharged by payment in due course by or on behalf of the drawee or acceptor.

'Payment in due course' means payment made at or after the maturity of the bill to the holder thereof in good faith and without notice that his title to the bill is defective.

(2) Subject to the provisions hereinafter contained, when a bill is paid by the drawer or an indorser it is not discharged; but

(a) Where a bill payable to, or to the order of, a third party is paid by the drawer, the drawer may enforce payment thereof against the acceptor, but may not re-issue the bill.

(b) Where a bill is paid by an indorser, or where a bill payable to drawer's order is paid by the drawer, the party paying it is remitted to his former rights as regards the acceptor or antecedent parties, and he may, if he thinks fit, strike out his own and subsequent indorsements, and again negotiate the bill.

(3) Where an accommodation bill is paid in due course by the party accommodated the bill is discharged.

Payment of a bill is generally made by the acceptor (or drawee). But in the case of dishonour, the holder can demand payment from any prior indorser or the drawer (section 57). Consequently a bill can be paid in due course by *any* party to a bill providing that party pays *the holder*, at or after maturity, in good faith and without notice that his title is defective (if defective it be). But, according to this section, a bill is discharged by payment in due course only where such payment is made by or on behalf of the drawee or acceptor. What then do we mean by the *discharge* of a bill?

If you repay a loan of £10 to your friend you *discharge* your indebtedness, i,e., the obligation ceases to exist and the transaction commencing with the original loan becomes finally closed. In the same way a bill is said to be discharged when the obligation it represents ceases to exist and all rights of action on the bill are extinguished. The obvious and most usual way of discharging a bill is payment in due course by the drawee or acceptor, and the whole transaction or series of transactions for which it has served as an instrument of payment are complete and settled. The bill becomes history, a mere voucher evidencing what has happened and how it was concluded. In short, it is no longer alive. To make certain that it remains *only* a voucher (and not misused in any other way) the drawee or acceptor may cancel the signature of the drawer. For example, where a banker pays a cheque drawn on him he cancels the drawer's signature as evidence of the discharge of the cheque and the latter remains a voucher to be used in his book-keeping.

Where the acceptor dishonours the bill the holder can enforce payment from any prior party. But payment in due course by an indorser or the drawer would not discharge the bill. If an indorser is compelled to pay the bill, he can likewise recover from a prior indorser or the drawer and in addition sue the acceptor for dishonour. If the drawer is compelled to pay, he can still sue the acceptor for dishonour. The main point is that the transaction which the bill represents is not complete whilst there remains a party liable on the bill and someone who can sue him. Payment of the bill leaving a party liable on it is NOT the discharge of the bill.

Observe that payment in due course is payment at or after maturity. Consequently, where an acceptor pays a bill *before* maturity (and he is quite free to do so), he can re-issue the bill, put it into circulation again by getting someone to give him value for it, and eventually pay it and discharge it when it matures. If in such circumstances the acceptor did *not* re-issue the bill but cancelled it in view of the fact that all parties were satisfied, would this amount to discharge of the bill? Yes. The bill would be discharged certainly—not by payment in due course, however, but by intentional cancellation (see section 63).

It is important to observe that payment in due course is payment to the HOLDER (see sections 2 and 24). We have observed from section 24 that no title to a bill can be obtained where an essential signature has been forged, that the person in possession of such a bill is not even a holder, and that the bill in fact belongs to the person whose signature has been forged. But the person in possession of the bill may be quite ignorant of the prior forgery and believe himself to be the holder and true owner. Whether he is ignorant of the forgery or not, he may still present the bill to the acceptor and obtain payment before the true owner discovers his loss. What is the position of the acceptor? Since he has not paid the holder he has not paid in due course; the bill is, therefore, not discharged and he can be compelled to pay again to the true owner (his only remedy is against the person he first paid). But if he pays the HOLDER, whether the latter is the true owner or not, he is *not* liable to the true owner.

Where a bill payable on demand (e.g., a cheque) is paid in due course by the drawee it is discharged and obviously cannot be re-issued.

Discharge of a cheque   This entails payment in due course by the drawee banker (i.e., the bank on which it is drawn) and only he can discharge it. (But see section 79 regarding crossed cheques.)

Subsection (3)   Accommodation bills are an exception to the general rule. Where the party accommodated pays the bill, he has no right of recourse to any other party and consequently the bill is discharged though not actually paid by the acceptor (section 28 refers).

60. Banker paying demand draft whereon indorsement is forged

Where a bill payable to order on demand is drawn on a banker, and the banker on whom it is drawn pays the bill in good faith and in the ordinary course of business, it is not incumbent on the banker to show that the indorsement of the payee or any subsequent indorsement was made by or under the authority of the person whose indorsement it purports to be, and the banker is deemed to have paid the bill in due course, although such indorsement has been forged or made without authority.

Under section 59 we saw that a drawee or acceptor who pays a bill to anyone but the holder remains liable to make payment again to the true owner. We saw too that he may quite innocently pay the wrong person and that the wrong person may be quite ignorant of his defect in or absence of title. Where it is a matter of only one bill there may be opportunity for a drawee or acceptor to make some enquiry and get confirmation that he is in fact paying the proper person. But before the passing of the Cheques Act 1958, we had the drawee banker paying hundreds and possibly thousands of cheques weekly with the obviously physically impossible task of making such enquiries in the case of each cheque. Such enquiries would have taken him in every part of this country and in many places abroad. He could not have ensured that every indorsement was genuine yet the forgery of one essential indorsement means that he is not paying the holder as section 59 requires. So section 60 was framed to relieve him of liability to the true owner of the cheque where an essential indorsement has been forged or made without authority, and it says that he is deemed to have paid the cheque in due course in any case providing he complies with the requirements of section 60, namely, good faith and ordinary course of business. Observe that this concession (or protection against the claims of the true owner) obtains only so far as *cheques* are concerned (i.e., cheques drawn on him by his own customers) and does not apply to other bills such as he may pay on behalf of his customer, the acceptor.

One of the fundamental features of the relationship between banker and customer is that there is an implied obligation on the part of the banker to pay his customers' cheques drawn on him providing they are in order, that sufficient funds have been provided by the customer or arrangement for overdraft sufficient to cover the cheques concluded, and that no legal bar exists. If a drawee banker refuses or delays payment without very good reason he will be liable in damages to his customer for injury to the latter's credit under breach of contract. Being placed in such a position as this, the paying banker, presented with a cheque drawn on him and a demand for its payment has no time allowed for enquiry as to the *bona fides* of the presenter unless there are circumstances that put the banker on enquiry in which case he could obviously delay payment.

Since the legislation of 1957, the Cheques Act, the significance of section 60 of this Act has diminished. The purpose of the 1957 Act was to eliminate as far as possible the indorsement of cheques and similar drafts drawn upon a banker. That legislation is discussed at the end of this volume. It is clear that the more successful the 1957 Act is, the less will this section 60 appear in importance since there cannot be a forged or unauthorised indorsement where there is no indorsement. Whilst indorsements continue to appear on cheques, the paying banker will still look to section 60 for his statutory protection against the consequences of paying on a forged or unauthorised indorsement. Since by agreement of the

London Clearing Bankers banks continue to insist on indorsements of cheques and like instruments paid in cash over the counter, as opposed to payment through the clearing house (a duty self-imposed since the Cheques Act allows for such payment without indorsement) then this practice, if pursued, will mean that section 60 can never die—it will be required to cover a bank paying cheques in cash over the counter. (It is argued in some quarters that section 60 never has covered the indorsement of the payee made prior to presentation of the cheque at the counter, it being submitted that such a signature is in the nature of a receipt rather than an indorsement. It is not the purpose of an elementary text book to pursue this fine point of law which in any case is very likely untenable and is best ignored for our study.)

Protection is given by section 80 to the drawee banker (generally known as the PAYING banker) in paying *crossed* cheques. These are presented to him by other bankers, generally through the banker's clearing. But section 60, and the Cheques Act 1957, apply also to crossed cheques. (But see sections 79 and 80 for additional duties incurred by a banker paying CROSSED cheques.)

Good faith   The reputation of British bankers is so sound that this factor is, of course, presumed.

Ordinary course of business   What this is can be determined only by recognised custom of bankers. For example, payment would not be in the ordinary course of business if it was made other than in bank hours. Again, a crossing on a cheque is a direction to the paying banker to pay the cheque only to another banker (who will be collecting the cheque in all probability for the holder). To pay a crossed cheque to an individual in cash over the bank counter would not be in the ordinary course of business and would be sufficient to deprive the paying banker of his protection under section 60. Except, of course, if he is paying the drawer personally on his cheque payable to 'Self'. Then, since there can be no question of paying the wrong person, he does not require the protection of section 60 or any other section. Whether the cheque is open or crossed here is quite immaterial. It is almost incomprehensible why some bank cashiers in such circumstances insist that the drawer 'open' or cancel the crossing before paying the cheque in cash.

It is worth noting, in analysing the wording of section 60 that the paying banker is not required to act without negligence, and a thing can be done negligently yet in the normal course of business.

Payment of cheques under advice   All banks today can make arrangements whereby their customers' cheques may be cashed by other branches of the bank and also by other banks. Where a bank pays under advice cheques drawn on another branch of the *same* bank, payment is considered to have been made by the drawee bank and section 60 will cover the branch making the payment.

Where, however, the cheques are cashed by another bank entirely, the cheques are NOT considered paid at all. The bank cashing the cheques is, in effect 'buying' them and, in normal cases, will be a holder for value (unless there has been forgery of an essential indorsement, etc.). If the bank gives cash for a cheque bearing a forged indorsement, it will have no title to the cheque and will be compelled to restore the cheque or its equivalent in money to the true owner. Section 60 will not apply since obviously, payment is not made by the bank on which the cheque is drawn.

Before leaving the subject of the payment of cheques under advice, it should be observed that the extension of section 60 to cover another branch of the same bank is considered to obtain only where arrangements have been made for the payment of cheques drawn on another branch. For example, if Maidenhead Branch of the Midland Bank paid an open cheque drawn on their Newcastle Branch, it would be protected by section 60 as regards that cheque only if the Newcastle Branch had previously made arrangements for the cheque to be paid at Maidenhead.

Payment of bills (other than cheques) by a banker   Although bills can be paid by the drawee or acceptor at his office or home, in practice most bills are 'domiciled with a bank' by the acceptor. That is to say, the drawee writes across the bill for his acceptance 'Accepted payable at Barclays Bank Ltd, Northborough', the bank at which his account is held, and the holder of the bill or his agent will present the bill there for payment on the due date. Although Barclays Bank Northborough is not obliged to pay its customer's 'domiciles' in the way that it is bound to pay the same man's cheques, yet the signature of the customer as acceptor is sufficient authority for the bank mentioned in the acceptance to pay the bill if it so decides. The danger, however, is that the bank cannot always be certain it is paying the holder—indorsements may have been forged—and should it not pay the holder the bank will be liable to compensate the true owner when he discovers his loss. Section 60 will not apply to such acceptances since they are not cheques. Consequently bankers could insist on a suitable indemnity from a customer before they pay his acceptances domiciled with them.

Having found that a bill can be discharged by payment in due course by the drawee or acceptor, payment of an accommodation bill by the party accommodated, and payment of cheques by the paying banker in accordance with section 60, we can proceed to sections 61, 62, 63 and 64 to observe other ways in which a bill may be discharged.

61. Acceptor the holder at maturity
When the acceptor of a bill is or becomes the holder of it at or after its maturity, in his own right, the bill is discharged.

This is fairly clear but few bills do, in fact finish their career in this way. There is a difference between this manner of discharge and payment in due course, for in this case there is no presentment for payment. An example would be in the case of a bill broker who, in purchasing a 'parcel' of bills, finds among them one of his own acceptances already due for payment.

62. Express waiver
(1) When the holder of a bill at or after its maturity absolutely and unconditionally renounces his rights against the acceptor the bill is discharged.

The renunciation must be in writing, unless the bill is delivered up to the acceptor.

(2) The liabilities of any party to a bill may in like manner be renounced by the holder before, at, or after its maturity; but nothing in this section shall affect the rights of a holder in due course without notice of the renunciation.

This is straightforward. But it is worth noting that although the renunciation or waiver would be effective if in writing without actual delivery of the bill to the acceptor, the latter is well advised to obtain the bill accompanied by the written waiver. Should he fail to do so, and the holder who renounced put the bill into circulation again so that it came into the hands of a holder in due course, the latter could compel the acceptor to pay the bill (unless there was evidence to show that the holder had notice of the waiver).

63. Cancellation

(1) Where a bill is intentionally cancelled by the holder or his agent, and the cancellation is apparent thereon, the bill is discharged.

(2) In like manner any party liable on a bill may be discharged by the international cancellation of his signature by the holder or his agent. In such case any indorser who would have had a right of recourse against the party whose signature is cancelled is also discharged.

(3) A cancellation made unintentionally, or under a mistake, or without the authority of the holder is inoperative; but where a bill or any signature thereon appears to have been cancelled the burden of proof lies on the party who alleges that the cancellation was made unintentionally, or under a mistake, or without authority.

It should be observed that whereas subsection (1) deals with the discharge of the *bill* by cancellation, subsection (2) concerns the discharge of a *party* from liability and *not* the discharge of the bill. (Compare section 64.)

Subsection (2) is made clear by an example.

A bill is drawn by A payable to B and goes by special indorsements from B to C, C to D, D to E, and E to F. F, the holder, is allowed to discharge from liability any party to the bill by merely striking out the signature of that party. Suppose F strikes out C's indorsement. C will not be liable again to any of the parties, the important fact being that no longer will he be liable to the subsequent parties D and E. If F can freely take away some of the rights of recourse of D and E, it is only fair that D and E should be relieved of liability to F. Thus, if F decides to release C from liability, he automatically releases D and E, the intermediate parties.

The main point of this section, though, is clearly expressed in subsection (1), viz., the discharge *of the bill* by intentional cancellation.

64. Alteration of bill

(1) Where a bill or acceptance is materially altered without the assent of all parties liable on the bill, the bill is avoided except as against a party who has himself made, authorised, or assented to the alteration, and subsequent indorsers.

Provided that,

Where a bill has been materially altered, but the alteration is not apparent, and the bill is in the hands of a holder in due course, such holder may avail himself of the bill as if it had not been altered, and may enforce payment of it according to its original tenor.

(2) In particular the following alterations are material, namely, any alteration of the date, the sum payable, the time of payment, the place of payment, and, where a bill has been accepted generally, the addition of a place of payment without the acceptor's assent.

Subsection (2) here gives examples of alterations considered 'material' but any alteration is material if it in any way, as Chalmers says, 'alters the operation of the bill and the liabilities of the parties, whether the change be prejudicial or beneficial . . .'. For example, subsection (2) does not include the alteration of the name of the drawee though this is a very important alteration particularly with cheques when drawee bankers (ill advisedly) alter them for re-direction to new bankers after an account has been transferred to another bank. Also, by virtue of the decision in *Lumsden & Co v London Trustee Savings Bank* ([1971] 1 Lloyd's Rep 114) it is now established that the name of the payee is also material.

A bill is *not* necessarily discharged by material alteration but certain parties can be discharged from their liability on the bill by reason of the alteration. (Compare subsection (2) of section 63.)

Example   A draws a bill for £8, payable to B. It is accepted by X and B negotiates it by special indorsement to C. C alters the bill to £80 and persuades D to give him £80 for it. The bill by special indorsements passes from D to E and from E to F. F presents it for payment on the due date but X refuses payment because of the alteration. What is the position of F? This depends on whether the alteration is apparent or non-apparent.

(1) Where it is apparent   The section says that the bill is avoided except as against a party who has made, authorised or assented to the alteration, and subsequent indorsers: meaning that F can still look to C and the subsequent indorsers, D and E for the £80 he gave for the bill. But he has no rights against those parties who did not make, assent to, or authorise the alteration, viz., A, B and X.

Nòte how similar this is to the rights of a person in possession of a bill on which an essential indorsement has been forged. He cannot sue the parties who signed prior to the forgery but he can sue all those who signed subsequent to it (section 55). This similarity is not surprising since a material alteration made to prejudice another person is included in the legal sense of forgery and punishable in a like manner as the same type of felony.

(2) Where it is non-apparent   (I.e., a clever alteration.) Here the holder is given *further* rights. Not only can he hold D and E liable for the full £80 as before but he can also hold A, B and X liable for £8 (the original tenor). In practice, therefore, B would claim his £80 from E and E similarly from D; D would be able to claim £80 from C if he could be found, but failing that £8 from A, B or X, thereby losing £72 by C's unauthorised alteration.

Alterations on cheques   Section 64 applies equally to cheques. In addition, the alteration of the word 'order' to 'bearer' (but not *vice versa*) and any deletion in the crossing would be considered a material alteration. If a cheque has been altered without the drawer's authority, the drawer is discharged from liability in accordance with this section, and the drawee bank would be unable to debit the drawer's account if it unwittingly paid such a cheque. If the alteration was a non-apparent alteration of the amount, the drawee bank would be entitled to debit the account with the original amount.

London Joint Stock Bank v MacMillan and Arthur (1918). The decision of the House of Lords in this case was of great importance to playing bankers. Until 1917, banks were continually incurring losses by clever alteration of cheques. The ease with which these alterations were made was often facilitated by the careless manner in which customers drew cheques. The House of Lords in 1918, however, ruled that *regarding cheques*, the drawer and not the bank must stand any loss occasioned by an alteration if the alteration and fraud were facilitated by the careless manner in which the cheque had been drawn, and that the customer owed a duty *to the bank* not to be negligent in this respect. (The drawer has no duty to others concerned with his cheque such as the payee or subsequent holders with the exception that emerged in the case of *Lumsden & Co v London Trustee Savings Bank* (above) when the court introduced the doctrine of contributory negligence. Lumsden & Co had drawn a cheque payable to 'Brown', which name stood for the full name of the payees 'Brown Mills & Co'. Since they had left sufficient space on the cheque in front of the name 'Brown' it was easy for a dishonest clerk to insert the initials 'J A G' before 'Brown' and convert the proceeds of the cheque to his own use. Though Lumsden & Co successfully sued the collecting bank for conversion, the court held that the drawers were partly responsible for the fraud in their lack of care in drawing the cheque. This is a most unusual (and the first) exception to the rule laid down in the *MacMillan* case. Lumsden & Co suffered a reduction in the amount of their claim. It is important to note that these decisions do not cover a customer's domiciles (i.e., bills accepted by the customer payable at his bank). There is still no obligation on the part of an acceptor to take the same care that is now demanded from him in his drawing of cheques.

Bank of England notes   Although section 64 applies equally to notes as to bills, it has been decided that Bank of England notes are an exception. Any alteration of such a note is deemed to vitiate the note completely whether the alteration be apparent or non-apparent. For example, a clever alteration of the number of a Bank of England note, made ostensibly to avoid its detection as a stolen note, has been held to make the note completely valueless to a subsequent holder.

Acceptance and Payment for Honour. [Sections 65–68]

65. Acceptance for honour supra protest
(1) Where a bill of exchange has been protested for dishonour by non-acceptance, or protested for better security, and is not overdue, any person, not being a party already liable thereon, may, with the consent of the holder, intervene and accept the bill supra protest, for the honour of any party liable thereon, or for the honour of the person for whose account the bill is drawn.

(2) A bill may be accepted for honour for part only of the sum for which it is drawn.

(3) An acceptance for honour supra protest in order to be valid must:

(a) be written on the bill and indicate that it is an acceptance for honour:

(b) be signed by the acceptor for honour.

(4) Where an acceptance for honour does not expressly state for whose honour it is made, it is deemed to be an acceptance for the honour of the drawer.

(5) Where a bill payable after sight is accepted for honour, its maturity is calculated from the date of the noting for non-acceptance, and not from the date of the acceptance for honour.

It can be visualised what inconvenience is caused to all parties, particularly the drawer, when the drawee refuses to accept the bill. The holder will probably reclaim from his transferor thus setting in motion a series of claims from transferee to transferor until the drawer eventually pays the payee. The whole process is the reverse of the original series of negotiations, etc., of the bill. It is to avoid this that the drawer sometimes indicates the name of a party to whom the bill should be presented 'in case of need' so that the bill can be accepted by someone if the drawee fails to accept. If such a person (the referee in case of need) does accept—though he is by no means obliged to—his acceptance is called an 'acceptance supra protest' or an acceptance for honour. The drawer would no doubt furnish the acceptor for honour with the necessary funds to pay the bill at maturity, in which case the acceptor for honour would be accepting for the honour of the drawer and would probably state so in his acceptance (e.g., 'Accepted S.P. for honour of drawer— Joseph Snell'). The acceptor for honour can likewise accept for the honour of an indorser. For instance, the payee may arrange such an acceptance to obviate the same prolonged proceedings on dishonour, and supply the acceptor for honour with funds to pay the bill at maturity. This would *not* interfere with or affect in any way his right to obtain payment from the drawer, afterwards. (See section 15.)

But it is important to note that besides a referee in case of need, ANYONE can accept a bill for honour providing they are not already liable on it.

N.B.:
(1) Like normal acceptances, an acceptance for honour can be for the whole of the amount of the bill or part thereof.
(2) Before such an acceptance can be taken, the bill must be pro-tested for dishonour by non-acceptance. (By virtue of section 93 it could be noted for the dishonour and the protest carried out later after the acceptance for honour.)
(3) The holder can refuse an acceptance for honour without pre-judicing himself in any way (but compare this with payment for honour, section 68).
(4) In the case of bills payable after sight and dishonoured by non-acceptance the maturity date is calculated from the date of protest (or noting) as section 14(3) provides notwithstand-ing a subsequent acceptance for honour.
(5) Note in the first sentence of this section the words 'or protes-ted for better security and is not overdue'. This is covered by section 51 (5).

66. Liability of acceptor for honour

(1) The acceptor for honour of a bill by accepting it engages that he will, on due presentment, pay the bill according to the tenor of his acceptance, if it is not paid by the drawee, provided it has been duly presented for payment and pro-tested for non-payment, and that he receives notice of these facts.

(2) The acceptor for honour is liable to the holder and to all parties to the bill subsequent to the party for whose honour he has accepted.

Observe that before the acceptor for honour will consent to pay the bill at its maturity, he must be given evidence that—
(a) The bill has been presented again to the original drawee, this time for payment, and that payment (like the acceptance before) was refused;
(b) The bill has been protested again, this time for non-payment.

67. Presentment to acceptor for honour

(1) Where a dishonoured bill has been accepted for honour

supra protest, or contains a reference in case of need, it must be protested for non-payment before it is presented for payment to the acceptor for honour, or referee in case of need.

(2) Where the address of the acceptor for honour is in the same place where the bill is protested for non-payment, the bill must be presented to him not later than the day following its maturity; and where the address of the acceptor for honour is in some place other than the place where it was protested for non-payment, the bill must be forwarded not later than the day following its maturity for presentment to him.

(3) Delay in presentment or non-presentment is excused by any circumstances which would excuse delay in presentment for payment or non-presentment for payment.

(4) When a bill of exchange is dishonoured by the acceptor for honour it must be protested for non-payment by him.

This section follows automatically on section 66 and requires no amplification.

68. Payment for honour supra protest

(1) Where a bill has been protested for non-payment, any person may intervene and pay it supra protest for the honour of any party liable thereon, or for the honour of the person for whose account the bill is drawn.

(2) Where two or more persons offer to pay a bill for the honour of different parties, the person whose payment will discharge most parties to the bill shall have the preference.

(3) Payment for honour supra protest, in order to operate as such and not as a mere voluntary payment, must be attested by a notarial act of honour which may be appended to the protest or form an extension of it.

(4) The notarial act of honour must be founded on a declaration made by the payer for honour, or his agent in that behalf, declaring his intention to pay the bill for honour, and for whose honour he pays.

(5) Where a bill has been paid for honour, all parties sub-

sequent to the party for whose honour it is paid are discharged, but the payer for honour is subrogated for, and succeeds to both the rights and duties of, the holder as regards the party for whose honour he pays, and all parties liable to that party.

(6) The payer for honour on paying to the holder the amount of the bill and the notarial expenses incidental to its dishonour is entitled to receive both the bill itself and the protest. If the holder does not on demand deliver them up he shall be liable to the payer for honour in damages.

(7) Where the holder of a bill refuses to receive payment supra protest he shall lose his right of recourse against the party who would have been discharged by such payment.

Just as a bill can be accepted for honour where it has been dishonoured by non-acceptance, so a bill can be paid for honour where the drawee or acceptor fails to pay it on its due date. But it should be made clear immediately that a payment for honour does NOT necessarily need a prior acceptance for honour although the one often follows the other.

Anyone can pay a bill for honour regardless of what has happened before, providing the bill has been dishonoured by non-payment and noted or protested—*anyone*, even though he is already liable on the bill (contract this with acceptance for honour, section 65). Legal proof of payment for honour should always be procured. This will be in the form of a 'Notarial Act of Honour', i.e., a document prepared by a notary, certifying that the payment for honour has been made, by whom, and for whose honour.

Subsection (5) can be explained by an example.

> A is the drawer, B, C, D, E and F are indorsers and G is the holder of a bill accepted but dishonoured by non-payment. X offers to pay it for the honour of C, and G takes the payment. D, E and F are, therefore, discharged from liability. X, however, obtains the rights to enforce payment from C and all the parties who would have been liable to C if C had paid the bill himself (viz., A and B and the acceptor Z).

In the same example, if a new person, Y, had offered to pay for the honour of the drawer, then Y's offer would have received preference over that of X since Y's payment for honour would have discharged B, C, D, E and F (see subsection (2)).

Subsection (7)   To continue the same example, if G, the holder, had refused the offer of X to pay the bill for honour (which, of course, he can do if he so chooses), then D, E and F would have been released from liability on the bill just as if the offer had been taken.

Lost Instruments. [Sections 69–70]

69. Holder's right to duplicate of lost bill

Where a bill has been lost before it is overdue, the person who was the holder of it may apply to the drawer to give him another bill of the same tenor, giving security to the drawer if required to indemnify him against all persons whatever in case the bill alleged to have been lost shall be found again.

If the drawer on request as aforesaid refuses to give such duplicate bill, he may be compelled to do so.

Note that the right of the person who was the holder to demand a duplicate from the drawer relates only to bills that are not over-due. But there is no right to demand that the other parties to the bill should sign the duplicate.

70. Action on lost bill

In any action or proceeding upon a bill, the court or a judge may order that the loss of the instrument shall not be set up, provided an indemnity be given to the satisfaction of the court or judge against the claims of any other person upon the instrument in question.

This section goes further than the preceding one. It allows the holder to sue any party to the lost bill whether the bill is overdue or not just as though the bill was available. A satisfactory indemnity must be furnished by the holder. In short, this section means that the loss of a bill shall not affect in any way the rights of the person who was the holder. This, of course, applies equally to promissory notes. A person who loses a Bank of England note has the right to demand a duplicate from the Bank, providing he supplies a suitable indemnity. The number of the lost note, of course, would have to be known.

Bill in a Set. [Section 71]

71. Rules as to sets

(1) Where a bill is drawn in a set, each part of the set being numbered and containing a reference to the other parts, the whole of the parts constitute one bill.

(2) Where the holder of a set indorses two or more parts to different persons, he is liable on every such part, and every indorser subsequent to him is liable on the part he has himself indorsed as if the said parts were separate bills.

(3) Where two or more parts of a set are negotiated to different holders in due course, the holder whose title first accrues is as between such holders deemed the true owner of the bill; but nothing in this subsection shall affect the rights of a person who in due course accepts or pays the part first presented to him.

(4) The acceptance may be written on any part, and it must be written on one part only.

If the drawee accepts more than one part, and such accepted parts get into the hands of different holders in due course, he is liable on every such part as if it were a separate bill.

(5) When the acceptor of a bill drawn in a set pays it without requiring the part bearing his acceptance to be delivered up to him, and that part at maturity is outstanding in the hands of a holder in due course, he is liable to the holder thereof.

(6) Subject to the preceding rules, where any one part of a bill drawn in a set is discharged by payment or otherwise, the whole bill is discharged.

Example

> £5,000   Nottingham
> 1 Jan 1983
> 90 days after date pay this first of exchange (second and third of the same tenor and date being unpaid) to the order of B Joyce & Co Ltd, the sume of five thousand pounds for value received.
> Richard Hedley
>
> To Carruel et Cie,
>   Toulon

When a bill is drawn in a set, the individual parts (in the example, three) form *one* bill. The wording of the second part will read '90 days after date pay this second of exchange (first and third of the same tenor being unpaid) to the order of, etc.' Similarly, the third copy will read '90 days after date pay this third of exchange (first and second of the same tenor and date being unpaid)'.

Such bills are used mainly in foreign trade. The main advantage is that copies can be sent by different mails. The loss of one part will not cause delay since *any part* can be accepted by the drawee. But the drawee should accept one part only. If he should sign his acceptance to say two parts he incurs the risk of having to pay twice should the two parts be negotiated to separate holders. As all the parts together form one bill they should be negotiated as a whole.

Even though the drawee accepts one part only, the holder of all parts could still (irregularly) negotiate the parts separately to different persons. One part would be in the form of an accepted bill and the others unaccepted. If this did happen, the acceptor should insist on paying the holder of the accepted part. If he paid an unaccepted part, he would no doubt be compelled to pay again when the accepted part was presented to him. Of course, a dishonest holder of all parts could negotiate the parts separately to different persons *before* any part was accepted. In this event, the holder who first gave value for his part is deemed to be the true holder of the entire bill. But the holders of the remaining parts may not lose their money since subsection (2) provides that the party who negotiated the parts separately and all persons who subsequently indorsed any part are liable thereon.

Example   *Bill in a set of three*

Drawer A
Payee B   } whilst all parts are held as one bill
Indorsee C

C negotiates the parts separately to D, G and K in that order of time.

Drawer	Indorser	Indorser	Indorser	Indorser	Holder
A	B	C	D	E	F
		C	G	H	J
		C	K	L	M

F is the true owner of the whole bill, but J and M can enforce payment from their prior parties back to C.

Conflict of Laws. [Section 72]

72. Rules where laws conflict

Where a bill drawn in one country is negotiated, accepted, or payable in another, the rights, duties, and liabilities of the parties thereto are determined as follows:

(1) The validity of a bill as regards requisites in form is determined by the law of the place of issue, and the validity as regards requisites in form of the supervening contracts, such as acceptance, or indorsement, or acceptance supra protest, is determined by the law of the place where such contract was made.

Provided that—

(a) Where a bill is issued out of the United Kingdom it is not invalid by reason only that it is not stamped in accordance with the law of the place of issue;

(b) Where a bill, issued out of the United Kingdom, conforms, as regards requisites in form, to the law of the United Kingdom, it may, for the purpose of enforcing payment thereof, be treated as valid as between all persons who negotiate, hold, or become parties to it in the United Kingdom.

(2) Subject to the provisions of this Act, the interpretation of the drawing, indorsement, acceptance, or acceptance supra protest of a bill, is determined by the law of the place where such contract is made.

Provided that where an inland bill is indorsed in a foreign country the indorsement shall as regards the payer be interpreted according to the law of the United Kingdom.

(3) The duties of the holder with respect to presentment for acceptance or payment and the necessity for or sufficiency of a protest or notice of dishonour, or otherwise, are determined by the law of the place where the act is done or the bill is dishonoured.

(4) Where a bill is drawn out of but payable in the United Kingdom and the sum payable is not expressed in the currency of the United Kingdom the amount shall, in the absence of some express stipulation, be calculated according to the rate of exchange for sight drafts at the place of payment on the day the bill is payable.

(5) Where a bill is drawn in one country and is payable in another, the due date thereof is determined according to the law of the place where it is payable.

The general rule laid down by this section is that where laws regarding bills of exchange differ from country to country, then whether an act, signature, etc., etc., is valid or not is determined by the law of the place in which it is done.

Exceptions

(1) Where a bill drawn abroad has not been correctly stamped as the laws of that country require, it will no doubt be invalid in that country. But it will *not* be treated as invalid by reason of this alone if it comes into the United Kingdom.
(2) A bill may be, in form, irregularly drawn abroad; nevertheless, if its form conforms with UK law it will be treated as valid as between all parties who negotiate it or hold it in the UK.
(3) Where an inland bill (i.e., a bill both drawn and payable in the UK) is negotiated abroad, the indorsements made abroad must conform with UK requirements.

One important effect on the general rule laid down here, was seen under section 24, viz., that if a forgery of an indorsement is made in a country where the law permits a person to obtain a good title to a bill in spite of the forgery, then if the bill is negotiated to a holder in the UK he also will get a good title.

In regarding subsection (4) here, reference should be made to section 9. Also it is interesting to note the case of *Barclays Bank International Ltd v Levin Bros (Bradford) Ltd* ([1976] 3 All ER 900). Here a bill expressed in foreign currency and payable in the UK was dishonoured by non-payment. Some months later a successful action was brought by the holder against the acceptor. In the interim, however, the rate for conversion of the bill into sterling had moved considerably against the plaintiff and of course in favour of the UK acceptor. It was held that the amount payable should in these circumstances be in the foreign currency of the bill. It is not clear what benefit is obtained by the holder since his conversion of the foreign currency into sterling which we must presume he wants will still be made at the same unattractive rate of exchange. And even if the holder is a foreigner, the sterling or the foreign-currency equivalent is patently the same.

Part III

Cheques on a banker. [Sections 73–82]

73. Cheque defined

A cheque is a bill of exchange drawn on a banker payable on demand.

Except as otherwise provided in this part, the provisions of this Act applicable to a bill of exchange payable on demand apply to a cheque.

Since a cheque is a certain narrow class of bills of exchange, a more detailed definition of a cheque can be obtained by amalgamating section 3(1) and this section. The result is:

> A cheque is an unconditional order in writing, signed by the person giving it, requiring the banker to whom it is addressed to pay on demand a sum certain in money to, or to the order of, a specified person or to bearer.

Nowhere in this Act is the word 'banker' defined precisely though section 2 does say that a banker is one who carries on the business of banking. But what precisely is the business of banking? How does it differ from mere money-lending? This is very important since a money-lender as such must register under the Moneylenders Acts or be unable to enforce repayment of his loans. If one's business is banking as we know it today then a certificate of the Board of Trade certifying that it is such is conclusive evidence.

74. Presentment of cheque for payment

Subject to the provisions of this Act:

(1) Where a cheque is not presented for payment within a reasonable time of its issue, and the drawer or the person on whose account it is drawn had the right at the time of such presentment as between him and the banker to have the cheque paid and suffers actual damage through the delay, he is discharged to the extent of such damage, that is to say, to the extent to which such drawer or person is a creditor of such banker to a larger amount than he would have been had such cheque been paid.

(2) In determining what is a reasonable time regard shall be had to the nature of the instrument, the usage of trade and of bankers, and the facts of the particular case.

(3) The holder of such cheque as to which such drawer or person is discharged shall be a creditor, in lieu of such drawer or person, of such banker to the extent of such discharge, and entitled to recover the amount from him.

Here, the drawer of a cheque is in a different position from the drawer of a bill, other than a cheque. Section 45 stated that delay in presentment of a bill for payment *discharged the drawer* and indorsers. Section 45 covered demand bills too, and said that if such a bill was not presented for payment within a reasonable time (and what that is, is determined by the nature of the bill, usage of trade and the facts of the case), *the drawer would be discharged*. But section 74 here says that if the demand bill is a cheque then the drawer is NOT automatically discharged by delay in presentment but only to the extent to which he has suffered actual damage or loss by the delay (though the *indorsers* would still be discharged by virtue of section 45).

> **Example**   A hands B a cheque for £1,000 in repayment of a loan. B does not present the cheque within a reasonable time and in the meantime, the bank goes into liquidation. The cheque now cannot be paid by the bank, whereas it would have been had there been no delay. Suppose the bank pays 50p in the pound. Now if section 45 operated. A would be completely discharged from his liability on the cheque, i.e., his loan would be deemed repaid, BUT he would obtain 50p in the pound from the bank's liquidators in lieu of the £1,000 not withdrawn. He would receive £500 and yet his indebtedness to B would be discharged. That is he would have suffered no loss by the delay and gained £500 in the process!! This was not considered equitable and thus the provision was made in this section that his debt to B shall be discharged only to the extent of the £500 lost in the bank's liquidation. The debt to B would be reduced to £500 which A would pay by handing him the £500 received from the bank's liquidators. The whole procedure could be arranged briefly by A's saying to B 'My debt is discharged by your delay but whatever the bank's liquidators may pay in respect of the £1,000, you can have.'

If no damage or loss is caused by unreasonable delay in present-ment of a cheque the drawer is liable on his cheque for 6 years from the date of the cheque, by virtue of the Limitation Act 1939.

N.B.—A holder of a cheque cannot present it to the drawee bank through the post—this can be done only between bankers themselves. This is because it is not customary for a holder of a cheque (other than the actual drawer himself) to present through the post. The use of the post for the purpose of presentment of *all kinds* of bills, including cheques, is permitted only where there is an established precedent (see section (8)).

75. Revocation of a banker's authority

The duty and authority of a banker to pay a cheque drawn on him by his customer are determined by:

(1) Countermand of payment;
(2) Notice of the customer's death.

Besides the two occasions mentioned here, a banker's authority to pay is terminated also by—

(a) Notice of lunacy of customer;
(b) Notice of presentation of a bankruptcy petition against him;
(c) Making of (Bankruptcy) Receiving Order (in the case of a Company, notice of its winding up);
(d) Assignment of balance by customer;
(e) Service of garnishee order attaching the whole of the balance;
(f) Notice that his customer is an undischarged bankrupt;
(g) Notice of a breach of trust (e.g., if it appears fairly certain that the cheque in question, drawn by a trustee, is a withdrawal of money to be used otherwise than for the purpose of the trust);
(h) Notice of defect in the presenter's title—this must obviously entail refusal to pay since a banker must pay in good faith;
(i) Where the customer's credit balance is insufficient to cover the cheque, or where the payment of the cheques would increase the customer's indebtedness above the agreed maxi-mum, the banker can pay or dishonour the cheques as he pleases;

It should always be borne in mind that the banker has a *duty* to pay his customer's cheques (unless circumstances such as those above operate), and a refusal to pay without adequate reason will mean the banker's being liable to his customer for damage to his credit. But in no circumstances will a banker be liable to the presenter of a cheque for wrongful refusal to pay or, in more technical terms, there is no privity of contract between the drawee banker and the holder of a cheque.

Countermand of payment (or 'stopping a cheque')   For this purpose, a banker requires the written and signed authority of his customer, the drawer, accompanied by a full description of the cheque (date, number, amount, payee's name, etc.). Where a banker receives such a request by telephone or telegram he must request written authority and until that arrives all he can do, if the cheque is presented, is to postpone payment pending confirmation.

If a cheque is received for payment through the bankers' clearing or by post from a banker or received over the counter for the credit of another customer's account, the drawer can stop payment any time up to the close of business that day, unless the banker has already specifically intimated that the cheque is paid.

But though a drawer has the right to prevent payment of his cheque by the drawee banker, he cannot thus deprive the holder of his rights to the cheque. If the holder of the cheque has a good title (e.g., a holder in due course) the drawer *himself* must pay if the bank returns the cheque 'stopped'. If the drawer should refuse, then the holder can sue him and compel him—
(a) to pay direct without the bank's ever seeing the cheque again, or
(b) to remove the 'stop' and enable the bank to pay.

Death or lunacy of a customer   Until the banker has received *reliable* notice of his customer's death or lunacy he can duly pay his customer's cheques. It is not the death or lunacy of the customer that terminates the duty to pay but the NOTICE of such. The balance in each case is held until it can be dealt with by the personal representatives of the deceased or by the customer's Receiver or Committee in Lunacy as the case may be. The notice must be reliable, but a banker would investigate any rumour, of course.

Crossed Cheques. [Sections 76–82]

76. General and special crossings defined
(1) Where a cheque bears across its face an addition of:

(a) The words 'and company' or any abbreviation thereof between two parallel transverse lines, either with or without the words 'not negotiable'; or

(b) Two parallel transverse lines simply, either with or without the words 'not negotiable';

that addition constitutes a crossing, and the cheque is crossed generally.

(2) Where a cheque bears across its face an addition of the name of a banker, either with or without the words 'not negotiable', that addition constitutes a crossing, and the cheque is crossed specially and to that banker.

In addition to the crossings receiving recognition here, there is another incorporating the words 'Account payee' which has received recognition by the courts and is an instruction to the collecting banker to collect only for the payee's account.

The words 'and Coy.' within the two parallel lines are a relic of early banking days and today are quite unnecessary.

General crossing

| (1) | (2) | (3) | (4) | (5) |

Special crossing

| (1) | (2) | (3) | (4) | (5) | (6) | (7) | (8) |

77. Crossing by drawer or after issue

(1) A cheque may be crossed generally or specially by the drawer.

(2) Where a cheque is uncrossed, the holder may cross it generally or specially.

(3) Where a cheque is crossed generally the holder may cross it specially.

(4) Where a cheque is crossed generally or specially, the holder may add the words 'not negotiable'.

(5) Where a cheque is crossed specially, the banker to whom it is crossed may again cross it specially to another banker for collection.

(6) Where an uncrossed cheque, or a cheque crossed generally, is sent to a banker for collection, he may cross it specially to himself.

Briefly, this section permits a holder besides the drawer to cross a cheque or add to a crossing in the ways it mentions. In addition, the payee could add 'Account payee' to a crossing.

Bankers collecting cheques for customers can cross them specially to themselves. In practice this they invariably do with a 'crossing stamp' in order to indicate to what bank the cheque must be returned if not paid by the drawee bank.

78. Crossing a material part of cheque

A crossing authorised by this Act is a material part of the cheque; it shall not be lawful for any person to obliterate or, except as authorised by this Act, to add to or alter the crossing.

This section adds to the effect of section 64 which defines and deals with the effect of material alterations on a bill. Section 64 applies equally to cheques as to bills but the section quoted here provides that, besides the items mentioned in section 64, the alteration of, the obliteration of, and the additions to a crossing on a cheque (except those additions permitted under section 77) shall also be considered as material alterations. Why was this not mentioned as part of section 64? Because bills, other than cheques, cannot be effectively crossed.

79. Duties of banker as to crossed cheques

(1) Where a cheque is crossed specially to more than one banker except when crossed to an agent for collection being a banker, the banker on whom it is drawn shall refuse payment thereof.

(2) Where the banker on whom a cheque is drawn which is so crossed nevertheless pays the same, or pays a cheque crossed generally otherwise than to a banker, or if crossed specially otherwise than to the banker to whom it is crossed, or his agent for collection being a banker, he is liable to the true owner of the cheque for any loss he may sustain owing to the cheque having been so paid.

Provided that where a cheque is presented for payment which does not at the time of presentment appear to be crossed, or to have had a crossing which has been obliterated, or to have been added to or altered otherwise than as authorised by this Act, the banker paying the cheque in good faith and without negligence shall not be responsible or incur any liability, nor shall the payment be questioned by reason of the cheque having been crossed, or of the crossing having been obliterated or having been added to or altered otherwise than as authorised by this Act, and of payment having been made otherwise than to a banker or to the banker to whom the cheque is or was crossed, or to his agent for collection being a banker, as the case may be.

Subsection (1)   A special crossing should mention one banker only and he is the banker who should collect the cheque for the holder. If it mentions more than one, the paying banker should refuse payment except where there are two bankers named in the crossing and one of them is a collecting agent for the other. Years ago, many provincial bankers (now absorbed by large banks) had no London office and were compelled to use the services of a London bank as agent for collecting cheques through the banker's clearing.

Subsection (2)   Briefly, this means that the drawee banker must pay a crossed cheque in accordance with the crossing. If he:
(a) Pays to anyone a cheque, that is crossed specially to two or more bankers;

(b) pays a cheque, that is crossed generally, to anyone other than
a banker;
(c) pays a cheque, that is crossed specially to anyone other than
the bank stated in the crossing,
then, in any of these cases, if payment is made to someone who is
not the true owner, the banker will be liable to the true owner. In
fact he will be compelled to make a second payment, this time to
the true owner. Of course, if he *does* pay the true owner, then it
matters nothing whether he paid in accordance with the crossing or
not. It is only when he does NOT pay the true owner that the
importance of this section arises.

Compare his position regarding open cheques. Section 59
directs that a bill (including open cheques) is discharged by payment in due course by the drawee or acceptor, payment in due
course being payment to the HOLDER, in good faith, etc., etc. If a
banker pays an open cheque to the HOLDER in accordance with section 59, he gets a valid discharge and is not liable even if the holder
is not the true owner. Further section 60 provides that even if he
does not pay the holder he will be considered to have paid in due
course if he complies with the requirements of that section.

If the cheque is crossed, however, the drawee banker has an
obligation either to—
(a) Pay the TRUE OWNER or
(b) Pay in accordance with the crossing.
Payment to the holder in accordance with section 59 is not enough
unless the banker pays as the crossing requires.

Example   A draws a cheque on X Bank, Sheffield, payable to B. B
receives the cheque and indorses it in blank. It is stolen from his pocket
by C. C takes the cheque, which is now payable to bearer, to X bank,
Sheffield and presents it for payment. The cheque is paid. The true
owner of the cheque, B subsequently sues the bank for wrongful conversion. What is the position? It depends entirely on whether the
cheque was open or crossed.

If cheque was uncrossed   The X bank is free from liability. C,
being the bearer is the holder of the cheque (see section 2). The
bank has paid the holder in good faith and without notice of defect
in his title—in short, it has discharged the cheque by payment in
due course in accordance with section 59. (Note: section 60 does
not apply here since no indorsement has been forged.)

If the cheque was crossed   The X bank is obliged to make payment in accordance with the crossing. The bank will still have paid the cheque in due course and discharged it, but the liability to the true owner remains, since the banker did not pay the true owner and failed to pay to another banker. (Note: the crossing, of course, could have been placed on the cheque by A or B—see section 77.)

From the above we conclude that although sections 59 and 60 apply equally to crossed as to open cheques, yet section 79 places an additional duty on the drawee bank in the payment of crossed cheques. He may make payment in due course and discharge the cheque, but if he has not paid the true owner and paid merely the holder, he will be liable to the true owner, *unless he has paid in accordance with the crossing*.

The effect of the above is, of course, that a banker on whom a crossed cheque is drawn will always pay in accordance with the crossing unless he is absolutely sure that the presenter is the true owner. Persons in possession of crossed cheques are perforce bound to employ a banker to obtain payment for them, i.e., they use a COLLECTING banker.

The rest of subsection (2) provides for tampering with crossings. If the drawee banker sees no evidence of this and pays the cheque as it appears to him to warrant, he will not be responsible for any loss that may be sustained by the true owner as a result of the unauthorised tampering with the crossing. For instance, a crossing may be entirely erased from a cheque by a clever thief and the cheque will appear to the drawee banker as 'open' and available for payment in cash. If he pays it to someone who is not a banker he will not be liable to the true owner (should he pay it to someone who is not the true owner) because he will have paid it in the normal way for open cheques.

General Summary and effect of sections 76–79

Cheques crossed generally   The drawee banker should pay to a banker. If he fails to do so, and at the same time pays someone who is not the true owner (even though he may pay the holder) he will be liable to recoup the true owner for his loss. On the other hand, if he fails to pay a banker and yet pays the true owner, he is perfectly safe. *The danger of not paying a crossed cheque to another banker arises only when the drawee banker does not pay the true owner.*

Cheques crossed specially   The drawee banker should pay only the banker mentioned in the crossing (or a banker acting as agent).

If he fails to do this and pays some other banker or some ordinary person and at the same time does *not* pay the true owner, he will be liable to recoup the true owner for his loss. As before, the danger arises only when he does *not* pay the true owner. If he *does* pay the latter, then it matters nothing whether the true owner was paid in cash personally or through a collecting banker.

It is not always correct to say that the drawee banker is failing to carry out his customer's instructions when he ignores the crossing. The crossing may not have been placed on the cheque by the customer, the drawer, since any holder of a cheque may cross it (see section 77), and a drawee banker has no duty towards any holder of a cheque unless the holder is the drawer. The main point is that if he ignores the crossing and pays the cheque not in accordance with the requirements of the crossing, he will be liable to the true owner unless the payment is made to the latter. No banker can afford to take this risk unless he is certain that he is, in fact, paying the true owner.

Observe the ways in which a banker can pay another banker:
(1) Through the bankers' clearings—banker pays by book entries;
(2) Direct presentation by post—banker pays by special book entries;
(3) Special presentation by nearby bank—banker pays by book entries or by cash;
(4) Payment to himself—this arises when one customer hands a cheque in for collection which is drawn on the same banker. The latter is then both paying and collecting banker.

80. Protection to banker and drawer where cheque is crossed
Where the banker, on whom a crossed cheque is drawn, in good faith and without negligence pays it, if crossed generally, to a banker, and if crossed specially, to the banker to whom it is crossed, or his agent for collection being a banker, the banker paying the cheque, and, if the cheque has come into the hands of the payee, the drawer, shall respectively be entitled to the same rights and be placed in the same position as if payment of the cheque had been made to the true owner thereof.

This section is somewhat similar to section 60 although it concerns only crossed cheques. The paying banker cannot be certain that the money he is paying for the crossed cheque to the collecting banker is being collected for the true owner. So, providing he pays:

(a) in accordance with the crossing:

(b) in good faith;

(c) without negligence,

he will not be liable to the true owner if payment is not received by the latter through the collecting banker.

Sections 60 and 80 compared

Section 60	*Section 80*
(1) Paying banker must pay in good faith	(1) Paying banker must pay in good faith.
(2) Paying banker must pay in the ordinary course of business	(2) Paying banker must pay without negligence.
(3) Indorsement must appear to be genuine. (This is of importance now, in view of the Cheques Act 1957, only where the cheque is 'open' and paid at the counter).	(3) No mention of indorsements, and in view of the Cheques Act 1957, a paying banker paying crossed cheques in accordance with the crossing is not concerned about them.
(4) Section 59 requires payment in due course (i.e., to the HOLDER). Banker is deemed to have made payment in due course (whether he has or not) if he fulfils section 60.	(4) Section 79 requires payment to the TRUE OWNER. Banker is deemed to have paid the true owner (whether he has or not) if he fulfils section 80.
(5) Banker can ignore section 60 if he has made payment in due course (i.e., to the HOLDER).	(5) Banker cannot ignore section 80 by paying in due course (to the HOLDER). He can ignore it only when he pays the TRUE OWNER.

The provisions of sections 79 and 80 concerning the payment of crossed cheques go further than sections 59 and 60. A drawee banker of crossed cheques is required to pay the true owner, not the holder, and only by complying with section 80 can he be safe from the claims of the true owner. It is *not* sufficient that he shall give a valid discharge of the cheque in accordance with section 59; he must pay the true owner or pay in accordance with section 80. Merely to make payment in due course without paying the true owner is not sufficient *unless section* 80 *is conformed with at the same time.*

(Section 80 also says that if a crossed cheque that the drawer sends to the payee in discharge of some obligation or debt reaches the payee then the debt, etc., is discharged no matter who subsequently obtains the cheque, *providing the cheque is eventually paid by the drawee banker.* For instance, the payee might indorse it in blank with a view to paying it in to bankers for collection and lose it before this can be done. The finder could probably obtain payment through a collecting banker before the loss was discovered. This is a general rule of law and requires little amplification. It is obvious that if you give your brother a pound note to repay a debt that you owe him, you cannot be called upon to pay again, if your brother loses the pound note.)

Crossings and the general public Why is it that a drawer crosses his cheque believing it to be a wise procedure? It is to make it difficult (though not impossible) for a thief to obtain payment. A thief who steals an open cheque can easily forge the necessary indorsement and present it to the drawee banker for payment before the loss is discovered. If the cheque is crossed then the thief must 'employ' a collecting banker to collect the cheque for him. He may not have a banking account (thieves rarely do) and so he would have to persuade someone who had an account to obtain the proceeds on his behalf. If the cheque were crossed specially, he would have even more difficulty since he would have to have an account with that banker or obtain assistance from some other person who had. It is true he may avoid all these difficulties, but in doing so, there must be some delay before the cheque is finally presented by a bank for payment. In the meantime it is very likely that the loss may be discovered and payment of the cheque be stopped by the drawer. Further, even if payment *is* obtained before the loss is discovered, the money is by no means lost, for it will be relatively simple to find for whom it was collected since doubtless such a person will be a customer of the collecting banker. Unless the cheque was payable to bearer when stolen, the person for whom it was collected, whether the actual thief or not, can be compelled to refund *notwithstanding that the cheque has been paid.* The fact that the cheque has been paid does not prevent action by the true owner to recover from the thief or anyone who assisted the thief to receive payment. The power remains with the true owner for six years after the date of payment.

N.B.—If the cheque was payable to bearer when stolen and the customer of the collecting banker had given value in good faith to the thief without notice of the theft he would be a holder in due course and the true owner of the cheque. In such circumstances the loser of the cheque could do nothing since he would no longer be the true owner.

Conversion   This term is used in a variety of ways, e.g., the exchange of securities for other securities or for cash. But its use in connection with negotiable instruments is to imply '*wrongful* conversion' which means the unauthorised dealing with another person's goods in such a way as to deprive him of possession. This covers not only thieves but also innocent 'agents' of thieves acting in complete ignorance of the previous conversion. Thus, a man who steals a cheque and cashes it is liable for conversion, but equally so is the banker who pays the thief. Again, if the cheque were crossed and the thief consequently used a banker to make collection, that banker, too would be liable for conversion. If the thief persuaded an innocent person to cash him the cheque and he paid it into his own banking account for collection, that person too, would be liable for conversion. The liability for conversion is always *to the true owner*. It lies in common law and covers all forms of property and all parties into whose hands the property comes. Consequently, when conversion of a cheque takes place and the true owner decides to take legal action, he can sue any, some or all of the parties who have been implicated (whether innocently or not). Obviously he is more likely to sue wealthy persons who have been implicated rather than poor ones. It is no use obtaining judgement for, say £1,000 against a poor man if he has no money to pay you! Consequently if banks have been innocently implicated, the true owner will often decide to sue them in view of their ability to pay if judgement is given against them. A parallel is seen in the case of libel printed in newspapers. The person prosecuting can sue not only the person who wrote the libel but also the printers, publishers, and wholesale newspaper distributors.

True owner   This expression is not defined anywhere in this Act. One is tempted to say that the meaning is obvious, but the law is not as easy as that. Who the true owner of a certain instrument is may have to be decided by the court when there is contention as to its ownership and its deliberations and decisions would be to determine, from the facts of the case, who had the best right, not only to the instrument itself, but also to the money flowing therefrom.

Under sections 60 and 80 of this Act and under the Cheques Act 1957 (section 1) we note the risk run by bankers in the payment of cheques drawn on them, the risk of having to make restitution to the true owner if they paid someone who had no right to the money. If the bank should refuse to make the restitution, the true owner might sue the bank, charging it with conversion. Thus the liability of a bank to the true owner of a cheque is a liability for conversion under common law. In all such actions, the only defence a bank can advance is some special statutory protection such as sections 60, 80 (and the Cheques Act—see later). It should be noted, however, that should a banker be compelled to make restitution to the true owner he has the right of recourse against the person for whom he acted. If he paid the thief or collected for the thief, the right of recourse may be of little value, for the thief, even if he has retained the money, may not be traced. But if the thief used some innocent person to approach the bank, then the bank's right of recourse against the latter may be of real value.

81. Effect of crossing on holder
Where a person takes a crossed cheque which bears on it the words 'not negotiable', he shall not have and shall not be capable of giving a better title to the cheque than that which the person from whom he took it had.

It will be recalled from the study of negotiable instruments that the essence of the word 'negotiable' was the facility to transfer by delivery a full legal title free from equities (including defects in title). We saw how a bill of lading was only transferable and not negotiable since any equity affecting one holder passed to the next holder when the bill of lading was transferred. To take away the negotiability of a cheque by adding the words 'not negotiable' is to put such a cheque in the category of 'Transferable instruments'. Thus if a thief finds a bearer cheque crossed 'not negotiable' and persuades an innocent person to give him cash for it, the innocent person cannot obtain any title to the cheque since, unless there is negotiability no title can be obtained through a thief. Even if the innocent person obtained payment of the cheque from the drawee banker, the true owner would have the right to demand restitution in money at any time within six years.

Obviously, the words 'Not negotiable' are added by the true owner of a cheque to obtain some advantage. What is this advantage, when is it obtained and who gets it?

If a normal cheque is payable to order, then the essential indorsement must be made before the title can be transferred. If the cheque is lost or stolen, the finder or thief must forge the essential indorsement before he can persuade someone to give him cash for it. The forgery will mean that no-one subsequently can obtain any right to the cheque (see section 24). But if the cheque is payable to bearer, then no forgery of indorsement will be necessary and the person who takes the cheque in accordance with section 29 will have a perfect title as a holder in due course in spite of the fact that the previous holder had no right to the cheque. But take away the negotiability and you ensure that where the cheque is drawn to bearer (or is an order cheque indorsed in blank) no-one can obtain a good title to the cheque should the true owner lose it. The advantage, therefore, is to preserve the rights of the true owner to a *bearer* cheque against any holder who takes the cheque subsequent to its theft or loss.

It should now be seen that the addition of the words 'Not negotiable' to a cheque payable to order is of no consequence if it is placed thereon to avoid the passage of title through a thief. The theft or loss of such a cheque would entail forgery of an indorsement and no-one would be able to get a good title against the true owner whether the words 'Not negotiable' appear on the cheque or not. The cheque is not in a 'Deliverable state' without the indorsement (see p. 22). But on a bearer cheque, the words give the true owner the same protection as if the cheque were payable to order. This does NOT mean that the 'Not negotiable' crossing turns bearer cheques into order cheques. A bearer cheque with the 'Not negotiable' crossing is *still* freely transferable by mere delivery and requires no indorsement.

Order cheques can be crossed 'Not negotiable' by the drawer, however, with another kind of contingency in mind. An example will make this clear. A agress that B shall do some work for him and hands him a cheque for £10 as part payment in advance. If B does not commence the work as arranged A can, and should quite properly, countermand payment of the cheque. Should B, however, have meanwhile negotiated the cheque to a holder in due course, C, A must see to it that C is paid the £10. But if the cheque had been crossed 'Not negotiable' when it was transferred to C then C's title could be no better than that of B, viz. defective.

The words 'Not negotiable' do not affect the drawee banker.

'Not transferable' cheques   (See section 8). These include:

(a) Cheques payable to a named payee followed by the word 'only';

(b) Cheques payable to a named payee and marked 'not transferable';

(c) *Uncrossed* cheques payable to a named payee and marked 'Not negotiable'. (Crossed cheques marked 'Not negotiable' within the crossing are of course fully transferable.)

By a Resolution of the London Clearing Bankers in May 1958 it was agreed that the drawing of non-transferable cheques would create serious difficulties for the banks and might expose them to risks which the committee decided should not be accepted. Customers of banks using such instruments were asked to discontinue the practice. The main reasons for the committee's decision were;

(1) A paying banker would have no statutory protection should such a cheque be cashed at the counter and positive identification of the payee would have to be made.

(2) The indorsement of the payee might in due course have become *prima facie* notice that the cheque had been transferred, and the paying banker, paying the cheque through the clearing house, would not be certain that he was carrying out his customer's mandate.

(3) A collecting banker could not become a legal holder for value of such a cheque and consequently would not be able to enforce payment in his own name.

(4) Difficulty would arise for payees who had no banking accounts. Collecting bankers would obviously have to collect only for the account of the payee.

(5) It is important to maintain the principle of transferability and negotiability of the cheque.

Before the drawer issues such a cheque to the payee, he is the true owner. When the payee receives it, he becomes the true owner. No other person, however, can take a full legal title. If the payee should transfer such a cheque then the title of the transferee would be an equitable one only—he would not be able to sue in his own name. Thus, bills and cheques marked 'Not Transferable' are still transferable under the rules of equity.

'Account-payee' crossings   These take the form of a crossing including the words 'Account payee' or 'Account payee only'. (A crossing with such words as 'Account John Martin' has a similar effect.) There is nothing in the Act to give statutory recognition of such a crossing but it is recognised by the courts as an instruction to the collecting banker to collect only for the payee, and any such banker ignoring these words does so at his peril. If he ignores the crossing and collects for someone who is not the payee, he is advised to make absolutely certain that such a person is the true owner of the cheque otherwise he will be liable to the true owner for conversion and by reason of his ignoring the words 'Account payee' he will no doubt lose the statutory protection available to him as a collecting banker in section 4 of the Cheques Act 1957. This is discussed later.

The words 'Account payee' do not concern the drawee banker who will treat the cheque as one crossed generally and pay to a banker. He cannot be saddled with the onerous task of ascertaining whether the collecting banker has conformed with the instruction or not. The words concern only the collecting banker. *They do not in any way limit the negotiability of the cheque.* The latter can be negotiated by the payee and pass from holder to holder and if a subsequent holder fulfilled the requirements of section 29 he would be a holder in due course of the cheque. He would certainly have some difficulty in persuading a bank to collect the cheque for him, but if this was met with then he could present the cheque to the drawer himself for payment and, if necessary, compel him to pay. Thus the protection that the 'account-payee' crossing gives to the true owner is very limited. If the cheque is indorsed in blank by the payee and then lost, the finder or thief can negotiate it to a holder in due course who will have a complete title to the cheque and rights to enforce payment by the drawer.

82. Protection to collecting banker
[Repealed by the Cheques Act 1957. The protection hitherto found in this section now springs from section 4 of the Cheques Act 1957 (see p. 175), which could be studied at this stage.]

Part IV

Promissory notes. [Sections 83–89]

83. Promissory note defined

(1) A promissory note is an unconditional promise in writing made by one person to another signed by the maker, engaging to pay, on demand or at a fixed or determinable future time, a sum certain in money, to, or to the order of, a specified person or to bearer.

(2) An instrument in the form of a note payable to maker's order is not a note within the meaning of this section unless and until it is indorsed by the maker.

(3) A note is not invalid by reason only that it contains also a pledge of collateral security with authority to sell or dispose thereof.

(4) A note which is, or on the face of it purports to be, both made and payable within the British Islands is an inland note. Any other note is a foreign note.

Observe how closely the definition of a note resembles that of a bill given in section 3. In fact most of the sections in this Act concerning bills (other than cheques) relate also to notes (see section 89).

It is interesting to note that an instrument promising the payment of money 'on or before 31 Dec 1956' was not held to be a valid promissory note by the Court of Appeal in *Williamson and Others v Rider* [1962] 2 All ER 268.

Subsection (2)   This is obvious after a moment's thought. Whilst the note is a promise by the maker to pay himself it is useless to anyone else. Once he indorses it the note becomes (by special indorsement) payable to someone else or (by blank indorsement) payable to the bearer. In either of these cases the maker becomes liable to someone if he delivers it, and thenceforward the note will act as a normal promissory note.

Subsection (4)   This is a guide as to what constitutes an inland note and what constitutes a foreign one. It is a parallel to section 4 regarding bills.

84. Delivery necessary
A promissory note is inchoate and incomplete until delivery thereof to the payee or bearer.

This is a parallel to section 21. As with the drawer of a bill, delivery is necessary in order that the maker shall be liable.

85. Joint and several notes
(1) A promissory note may by made by two or more makers, and they may be liable thereon jointly, or jointly and severally according to its tenor.

(2) Where a note runs 'I promise to pay' and is signed by two or more persons it is deemed to be their joint and several note.

Examples of a joint note

```
£700                              Leicester
                                 1 Jan 1983
Ninety days after date we promise to pay William
Smith or order the sum of seven hundred pounds.
                         James Harrison
                         John Martin
                         Florence Brown
```

Examples of joint and several note

```
£1,000                              Derby
                                 1 Jan 1983
Six months after date we jointly and severally promise
to pay the bearer the sum of one thousand pounds.
                         Frank Scott
                         Leslie White
```

```
£200                            Birmingham
                                 1 Jan 1983
I promise to pay to the order of John Davies on
demand the sum of two hundred pounds.
                         George Hallam
                         John Douglas
                         Charles Harrison
```

What is the difference between a joint note and a joint and several note? As far as the makers are concerned there is little. Whether they undertake joint liability or joint and several, each maker is *individually* liable for the FULL amount of the note, and if called on to pay, he must pay the holder the whole amount involved. He cannot say 'Three of us signed the note so here is my third share'. He must pay the whole amount and afterwards it is his concern to obtain from his fellow-makers whatever is their share of the liability. The only difference as far as the makers are concerned is that in the case of a joint note, the death of a maker extinguishes the liability as far as he is concerned and the holder of the note will have no claim against the deceased maker's personal representatives.

The main point of difference concerns the holder of the note in the event of the makers' refusal to pay. In such an event he can sue the makers and enforce payment. If the note is joint and several he can sue each one of the makers in turn. For example, if Smith, Jones and Brown are the makers of a joint and several note, the holder may decide to sue Smith alone. He will probably win his case and obtain an order of the Court against Smith. But, supposing Smith becomes bankrupt immediately, and pays one penny in the pound, then the holder can sue one of the remaining makers (say Jones) for the amount unpaid. If the same fate overtakes Jones, the holder can bring a third action in court and sue Brown for the remainder. Of course, if he so chooses, he can sue two jointly or all three makers together.

The power to bring separate actions against each maker is, however, denied to the holder of a joint note. He has only one right of action, i.e., he can sue in court but once. He can sue one maker alone, or sue some but not all of the makers, or sue all the makers together. But if he fails to obtain satisfaction by his action in court he will be allowed no second attempt. Thus if he sues only one maker or some but not all of them and fails to recover the full amount of the note, he will be unable to sue any maker who was not included in the action. Consequently he would be foolish not to sue *all* the makers in his one action.

In more technical language, we can say that in the case of a joint note there is only one debt and, therefore, only one right of action, but in the case of a joint and several note, there are as many debts as there are makers and, therefore, as many rights of action as there are makers. But a holder is not allowed to recover more than the full amount of the note.

86. Note payable on demand

(1) Where a note payable on demand has been indorsed, it must be presented for payment within a reasonable time of the indorsement. If it be not so presented the indorser is discharged.

(2) In determining what is reasonable time, regard shall be had to the nature of the instrument, the usage of trade, and the facts of the particular case.

(3) Where a note payable on demand is negotiated, it is not deemed to be overdue, for the purpose of affecting the holder with defects of title of which he had no notice, by reason that it appears that a reasonable time for presenting it for payment has elapsed since its issue.

This is a parallel to section 45. Like demand bills, demand notes must be presented for payment within a reasonable time. But it should be observed that whereas delay in presentation of a demand bill (other than cheque) will discharge the indorsers *and* the drawer, the delay with a demand note will discharge only the indorser and *not* the maker(s) (unless the delay is six years or more after the date of the note, in which case the Limitation Act 1939, will release all parties).

Subsection (3) of this section places the holder of a demand note in a better position than a holder of a demand bill. According to section 29, a holder in due course must take the bill before it is overdue—if he takes an overdue bill he is affected by prior equities even though he has no knowledge of them. But a person can be a holder in due course of a demand note even though it appears overdue at the time it is negotiated to him. Compare section 36(3).

87. Presentment of note for payment

(1) Where a promissory note is in the body of it made payable at a particular place, it must be presented for payment at that place in order to render the maker liable. In any other case, presentment for payment is not necessary in order to render the maker liable.

(2) Presentment for payment is necessary in order to render the indorser of a note liable.

(3) Where a note is in the body of it made payable at a particular place, presentment at that place is necessary in order to render an indorser liable; but when a place of payment is indicated by way of memorandum only, presentment at that place is sufficient to render the indorser liable, but a presentment to the maker elsewhere, if sufficient in other respects shall also suffice.

This section is fairly straightforward. It should be observed that a maker of a note remains liable on it for 6 years after its maturity even though presentment for payment is not made. Obviously, however, the presentment for payment must be made before an indorser is liable for payment. In other words, before an indorser can be compelled to pay he must be satisfied that the holder has endeavoured to obtain payment from the party primarily liable for payment (viz., the maker). Thus the liability of an indorser of a note is parallel to that of an indorser of a bill (see section 45).

88. Liability of maker
The maker of a promissory note by making it:
   (1) Engages that he will pay it according to its tenor;
   (2) Is precluded from denying to a holder in due course the existence of the payee and his then capacity to indorse.

This is somewhat similar to the liability of an acceptor of a bill, see section 54.
   Subsection (1) here is obvious.
   Subsection (2) provides that the maker cannot escape liability by pleading that the holder has no title because the payee (from whom the holder normally derives his title) is non-existent, etc. If a maker could do this then the opportunity for fraud appears obvious.

89. Application of Part II to notes
(1) Subject to the provisions in this part, and except as by this section provided, the provisions of this Act relating to bills of exchange apply, with the necessary modifications, to promissory notes.

(2) In applying those provisions the maker of a note shall be deemed to correspond with the acceptor of a bill, and the first indorser of a note shall be deemed to correspond with the drawer of an accepted bill payable to drawer's order.

(3) The following provisions as to bills do not apply to notes; namely, provisions relating to:

(a) Presentment for acceptance;

(b) Acceptance:

(c) Acceptance supra protest;

(d) Bills in a set.

(4) Where a foreign note is dishonoured, protest thereof is unnecessary.

The word 'part' in subsection (1) means Part 4 of the Act, viz., sections 83 to 89.

From this section we see that the Act applies equally to notes as to bills, except as laid down in sections 83–89.

Observe that a foreign note needs no protest on dishonour whereas a foreign bill must be protested on dishonour or the drawer and indorsers will be discharged from liability (see observations on section 5 (2)).

Résumé on promissory notes

The difference between a bill and a note can be tabularised.

Bill	*Note*
(1) Where payable after date, a bill is generally accepted.	(1) Never accepted.
(2) Where payable after sight, a bill must be presented for acceptance to fix the maturity date of the bill, and presentment for acceptance is necessary to render the prior parties liable.	(2) Never accepted.
(3) Can be accepted for honour.	(3) Never accepted.
(4) Can be drawn in a set.	(4) Cannot be drawn in a set.
(5) Foreign bills need protesting on dishonour to retain the liability of prior parties.	(5) Protest is never needed.

(6) Before acceptance, the drawer is primarily liable for payment, but after acceptance the acceptor becomes primarily liable for payment.
(7) Where there are two or more acceptors of a bill drawn on joint drawees, the acceptors are always jointly liable.
(8) An acceptance can be conditional.
(9) A bill is an order to pay.

(6) Maker is always the party liable primarily for payment.
(7) Where there is more than one maker, they can be liable jointly or jointly and severally according to the terms of the note.
(8) The promise to pay can never be conditional
(9) A note is a promise to pay.

Bank notes   These are promissory notes issued by a bank engaging to pay the bearer on demand whatever sum is expressed in the note. Since they are used as currency, the fact that they are promissory notes and governed by the Bills of Exchange Act 1882, is often overlooked. A transferor of a bank note, for example, is affected by section 58 equally as if a transferor of a bearer bill. But one point of difference is worth observing. Section 64 provides that where a material alteration on a bill is *not* apparent, the drawer and all indorsers who signed prior to the alteration are still liable for the original tenor of the bill. Any alteration of a bank note, however, renders the note entirely void as against the issuing bank whether the alteration is apparent or not (*Suffell v Bank of England* (1882)).

If a Bank of England note is stolen or lost, a stop can be placed at the Bank by the loser for a small fee. This has the effect of allowing the Bank of England to postpone payment of the note if and when it is presented for payment. But if the enquiries made subsequently show that the presenter is a *bona fide* holder for value, the Bank has no option but to pay and the loss will fall on the original loser of the note. The value of a 'stop' on a Bank of England note is consequently very doubtful. Almost all Bank of England notes presented to the Bank for payment are from large commercial banks in their withdrawal of soiled notes from circulation who will be holders for value.

Sections 69 and 70 regarding lost bills apply of course to bank notes. Where one is lost or destroyed a duplicate can be demanded from the Bank of England, providing a satisfactory indemnity is provided. (Similarly with notes issued by banks in Scotland and Northern Ireland.)

Part V

Supplementary. [Sections 90–100]

90. Good faith
A thing is deemed to be done in good faith within the meaning of this Act, where it is in fact done honestly, whether it is done negligently or not.

This was dealt with earlier under 'Good faith' (see p. 21).

91. Signature
(1) Where, by this Act, any instrument or writing is required to be signed by any person it is not necessary that he should sign it with his own hand, but it is sufficient if his signature is written thereon by some other person by or under his authority.

(2) In the case of a corporation, where, by this Act, any instrument or writing is required to be signed, it is sufficient if the instrument or writing be sealed with the corporate seal.

But nothing in this section shall be construed as requiring the bill or note of a corporation to be under seal.

This is fairly obvious. Note, however, that whereas companies generally incur liability on a document by placing the company's seal thereon, this is not necessary in the case of bills or notes. For example, the signature of a director, duly authorised to sign for the company, will suffice to bind the company as a party to a bill or note.

92. Computation of time
Where, by this Act, the time limited for doing any act or thing is less than three days, in reckoning time, non-business days are excluded.

'Non-business days' for the purposes of this Act mean:
(a) Sunday, Good Friday, Christmas Day;

   (b) A bank holiday under the Bank Holidays Act 1871, or
       Acts amending it;
   (c) A day appointed by Royal proclamation as a public
       fast or thanksgiving day.

With the closing of banks on Saturdays came the Banking and
Financial Dealings Act 1971 to make Saturdays non-business days.
During 1982 one commercial bank began the provision of simple
personal banking services on Saturdays for 'non-business' customers. The Act of 1971 still stands, however, and Saturdays remain
officially non-business days.

   Any other day is a business day.

   This is closely concerned with section 14 regarding the calculation of the due date of a bill.

93. When noting equivalent to protest

For the purposes of this Act, where a bill or note is required to
be protested within a specified time or before some further
proceeding is taken, it is sufficient that the bill has been noted
for protest before the expiration of the specified time or the
taking of the proceeding; and the formal protest may be
extended at any time thereafter as of the date of the noting.

This section should be read in conjunction with section 51. It is the
authority for 'noting' a dishonoured bill and thereby empowering
the holder to make the formal protest at any time subsequently.

94. Protest when notary not accessible

Where a dishonoured bill or note is authorised or required
to be protested, and the services of a notary cannot be
obtained at the place where the bill is dishonoured, any
householder or substantial resident of the place may, in the
presence of two witnesses, give a certificate, signed by them,
attesting the dishonour of the bill, and the certificate shall in
all respects operate as if it were a formal protest of the bill.

   The form given in Schedule I to this Act may be used with
necessary modifications, and if used shall be sufficient.

The first Schedule to this Act runs as follows:

FIRST SCHEDULE

Form of protest which may be used when the services of a notary cannot be obtained.

Know all men that I, A.B. (householder), of
in the county of   in the United Kingdom, did on
the   day of   188   at   demand
payment (or acceptance) of a bill of exchange hereunder written
from E.F., to which demand he made answer (state answer, if
any) wherefore I now, in the presence of G.H., and J.K., do
protest the said bill of exchange.

(Signed)   A.B.

G.H.

J.K.   Witnesses

N.B.—The bill itself should be annexed, or a copy of the bill
and all that is written thereon should be underwritten.

95. Dividend warrants may be crossed

The provisions of this Act as to crossed cheques shall apply
to a warrant for payment of dividend.

A dividend warrant is defined as a demand draft drawn by a company on a banker payable to a stockholder or shareholder and representing his share in the profits of the company. Dividend warrants years ago sometimes failed to be valid cheques by reason of a technical point (e.g. they were sometimes drawn on alternative drawee banks and section 6 says that such documents cannot be valid bills). Section 95 here was accordingly included to provide banks with the statutory protection available in the crossed-cheque sections when handling such documents as though they were valid cheques. Since section 60 was *not* extended by virtue of this section. Banks paying open dividend warrants had to look to section 19, Stamp Act 1853 which is similar in effect to section 60 above but wider in scope and included 'any draft or order' whether it was a valid cheque or not. See p. 191.

Today however almost every dividend warrant used is in fact a valid cheque. In any case, by virtue of the Cheques Act 1957, the discharge of the payee on a dividend warrant is no longer required and current designs of such warrants indicate this. Consequently, bankers paying or collecting dividend warrants, whether they are valid cheques or not, are protected by the Cheques Act 1957, which see.

Interest warrants   These differ from dividend warrants in that they are used for the payment of *interest* on money *lent* (e.g. Debenture Interest). Although the judgment in the case of *Slingsby v Westminster Bank* (1930) stated that section 95 was intended to cover interest warrants re Government Stock as well as dividend warrants, the matter is not considered settled law yet, this being the only case of its kind so far before the courts.

The point now is academic since the Cheques Act is so framed to include all such documents as these and bankers have the same protection as though they were valid cheques.

96. [*This section was repealed in* 1898.]

97. Savings
(1) The rules in bankruptcy relating to bills of exchange, promissory notes, and cheques, shall continue to apply thereto notwithstanding anything in this Act contained.

(2) The rules of common law including the law merchant, save in so far as they are inconsistent with the express provisions of this Act, shall continue to apply to bills of exchange, promissory notes, and cheques.

(3) Nothing is this Act or in any repeal affected thereby shall affect
   (a) Any law or enactment for the time being in force relating to the revenue;
   (b) The provisions of the Companies Act 1862, or Acts amending it, or any Act relating to joint stock banks or companies;
   (c) The provisions of any Act relating to or confirming the privileges of the Bank of England or Bank of Ireland respectively;
   (d) The validity of any usage relating to dividend warrants, or the indorsements thereof.

This means that the Act is not intended to supersede anything in the law relating to bankruptcy, but whilst providing that common law including the Law Merchant still applies to bills and notes, it stipulates that where common law and the Bills of Exchange Act 1882, conflict, then the latter shall prevail. For example, we have seen how sections 60 and 80 override common law and provide a banker with protection against their normal common-law liability for conversion.

Observe subsection (3)(d). This, in effect, recognises the custom whereby the signature of one payee only was sufficient discharge for a dividend warrant payable to joint payees (but *interest* warrants on the other hand, payable to two or more payees were discharged by all the payees). See Cheques Act 1957, p. 172, for abolition of discharge.

Sections 98, 99 and 100 of this Act are of no importance to the student of banking law.

Part 3
Cheques Act 1957

Cheques Act 1957

This Act was the culmination of years of pressure from several quarters to eliminate the indorsement of cheques. The cheque by 1957 had long since been forgotten by most people as an instrument to be freely transferred (which of course it was and still is) since the life of almost every cheque issued had become brief—it rested but a short time in the payee's hands and then in almost every case proceeded from him to the collecting bankers for collection. It has ceased in practice to be an instrument of transfer and is now by usage looked upon rather as a mandate or authority given by the drawer to his banker to pay from his account the amount of the cheque, in which case the indorsement of the payee is not placed thereon for the purpose of transfer and passage of title but rather to effect a discharge of the instrument. The abolition of the indorsement of the payee in such circumstances (i.e., where there is no transfer of the cheque by the payee to an indorsee) appeared before 1957 a practical proposition and worthy of legislation with the main object of saving time particularly for those institutions receiving thousands of cheques in the course of a few days. In consequence of the modern approach to the use of the cheque the Cheques Act 1957, was born. The supporters of the Act no doubt also had in mind the amount of work to be avoided inside the banks in the examination of indorsements and the dishonour of cheques for irregularities. It is equally important to note that opportunity was taken at the same time to do some tidying-up and improvement with the existing legislation concerning the protection of bankers against their common law liability for conversion in their handling of cheques and similar documents.

1. Protection of bankers paying unindorsed or irregularly indorsed cheques

(1) Where a banker in good faith and in the ordinary course of business pays a cheque drawn on him which is not

indorsed or is irregularly indorsed, he does not, in doing so, incur any liability by reason only of the absence of, or irregularity in, indorsement, and he is deemed to have paid it in due course.

(2) Where a banker in good faith and in the ordinary course of business pays any such instrument as the following, namely:

(a) a document issued by a customer of his which, though not a bill of exchange, is intended to enable a person to obtain payment from him of the sum mentioned in the document;

(b) a draft payable on demand drawn by him upon himself, whether payable at the head office or some other office of his bank;

he does not, in doing so, incur any liability by reason only of the absence of, or irregularity in, indorsement, and the payment discharges the instrument.

The paying banker   These two subsections could have been drafted as one. In each case the paying banker is required to act in good faith and in the ordinary course of business. If he does, then any demand draft on that banker that is a mandate for him to pay some named payee is validly discharged by his payment even though the indorsement is missing or is irregular. Such drafts include cheques, dividend warrants and banker's drafts.

An irregular indorsement must not be confused with a forged one. With the former we have in mind a genuine signature placed on the instrument by the proper person or his authorised agent which does not conform with banking custom. A simple case occurs where a cheque payable to John Fox is indorsed by that person 'John E Fox'.

The protection of the paying banker paying under a forged or unauthorised indorsement by reason of this new Act is not now entirely clear. We saw under section 24 of the Act of 1882 that a forged or unauthorised signature is wholly inoperative and equivalent to a blank on the paper. If such doctrine is allied with the provisions of section 1 of the Cheques Act 1957, it may well be argued that the latter section will protect such a banker since the instrument is at law tantamount to an unindorsed instrument. If this argument is not valid (and we must wait perhaps for a High Court ruling) then the protection of drawee bankers paying under forged or unauthorised indorsements will be resolved as follows:

	Open	*Crossed*
Cheques	60, BE Act 1882	Ss. 60 and 80, BE Act 1882
Banker's drafts	19, Stamp Act 1853	S. 19, Stamp Act 1853 and s. 80 of BE Act 1882 by virtue of s. 5, Cheques Act 1957.
Conditional orders	None	S. 80, of BE Act 1882 by virtue of s. 5, Cheques Act 1957.

In any case we noted under section 60 of the 1882 Act, that in spite of the opportunity given by the Cheques Act 1957, to abolish indorsements completely, bankers still insist on the indorsement of the payee where payment is made at the counter in cash. In consequence, we still look to section 60 of the 1882 Act for protection where in these circumstances payment is made against a forged or unauthorised indorsment. What would be the effect of failing to obtain an indorsement where someone not entitled to the cheque presented it for payment? This would not be payment in the 'ordinary course of business' and the banker would be without protection.

Before 1957 there had been a growing practice with companies, local authorities and the like to require the completion of a receipt by the payee on the cheque as a prerequisite to payment. In the spirit engendered by the Cheques Act 1957, to abolish indorsements, most of these receipts have been dispensed with, the drawer relying on section 3 of the Act which states that an unindorsed cheque paid by the drawee banker is evidence of receipt by the payee. A few such customers of banks, however, still insist on the payee's receipt and such cheques are marked with a bold capital letter 'R' on the face, and the relative drawee bankers are still required to ensure that the receipt is duly completed before they make payment. Failure to ensure this would not be payment in the ordinary course of business, and if the question of conversion arises, it would appear that the paying banker concerned would have no statutory protection from his liability to the true owner. In any case he would certainly be guilty of non-compliance with his customer's mandate and be liable to him for any loss he may suffer thereby. Banks strongly discourage the practice.

2. Rights of bankers collecting cheques not indorsed by holders

A banker who gives value for, or has a lien on, a cheque payable to order which the holder delivers to him for collection without indorsing it, has such (if any) rights as he would have had if, upon delivery, the holder had indorsed it in blank.

We shall see under section 4 that in certain circumstances a banker taking a cheque or similar instrument for collection may find himself collecting as a holder for value. In normal circumstances where the instrument in point is payable to order, the latter's indorsement would of course be necessary for transfer. Since by virtue of section 4 of this Act, cheques etc. are unlikely to be indorsed when handed in for collection, this section 3 is included to enable a bank to take title, other factors being in order, in spite of the absence of the 'essential' indorsement. This of course is an exception to section 31 of the 1882 Act and is obviously peculiar to banks alone. This concession, however, will not enable him to take title through a thief since the section states clearly that the banker must receive the cheque from *the holder*.

The first case to be decided under this section was that of *Barclays Bank Ltd v Harding* where the bank successfully established that it was a holder in due course notwithstanding that the holder of the cheque had not endorsed it before transfer to the bank.

It should be observed that this section speaks only of *cheques*. It does not include analogous instruments that are not strictly valid bills of exchange; yet section 4(2) of this Act enables a collecting banker to collect a variety of instruments other than valid cheques and be unprejudiced by their lacking indorsement. There appears to be some inexplicable inconsistency here. One cannot understand why the law has been drafted so that a collecting banker collecting unindorsed cheques and unindorsed analogous instruments as a collecting agent can subsequently in case of need plead holder for value in the case of the valid cheques but must fail in the case of the analogous instruments.

There is another aspect of this section that causes bankers some misgivings. It speaks of the *absence* of indorsement of a cheque not to upset a collecting banker who attempts to plead holder for value—it says nothing of cheques irregularly indorsed and the conclusion is that such an irregularity may still today, as before 1957, prevent his taking a good title. In this Act we note that sections 1 and 4 provide for cheques and analogous instruments, for unindorsed and irregularly indorsed instruments always without prejudice either way. Yet section 2 above mentions but unindorsed cheques, not unindorsed analogous instruments, not irregularly indorsed cheques, not irregularly indorsed analogous instruments

3. Unindorsed cheques as evidence of payment
An unindorsed cheque which appears to have been paid by the banker on whom it is drawn is evidence of the receipt by the payee of the sum payable by the cheque.

Before 1957, the drawer of a cheque could always use it after payment by his bankers as *prima facie* evidence of receipt by the payee of the sum payable. This section merely brings the matter up to date and provides that whereas before 1957 the indorsed paid cheque was good evidence, now the unindorsed cheque is similarly good evidence. Why the public seized on this section in 1957 as an excuse to dispense with separate receipts is strange. The opportunity had been there long before 1957 to make use of the paid cheque for this purpose.

If the order to pay is not drawn strictly in accordance with the requirements of a valid cheque (an analogous instrument) then it would appear that unindorsed and paid by the banker it would *not* be evidence of receipt since this section speaks only of unindorsed *cheques*.

4. Protection of bankers collecting payment of cheques, etc.
(1) Where a banker, in good faith and without negligence—
   (a) receives payment for a customer of an instrument to which this section applies; or
   (b) having credited a customer's account with the amount of such an instrument, receives payment thereof for himself;

and the customer has no title, or a defective title, to the instrument, the banker does not incur any liability to the true owner of the instrument by reason only of having received payment thereof.

(2) This section applies to the following instruments, namely—

(a) cheques;

(b) any document issued by a customer of a banker which, though not a bill of exchange, is intended to enable a person to obtain payment from that banker of the sum mentioned in the document;

(c) any document issued by a public officer which is intended to enable a person to obtain payment from the Paymaster General or the Queen's and Lord Treasurer's Remembrancer of the sum mentioned in the document but is not a bill of exchange;

(d) any draft payable on demand drawn by a banker upon himself, whether payable at the head office or some other office of his bank.

(3) A banker is not to be treated for the purposes of this section as having been negligent by reason only of his failure to concern himself with absence of, or irregularity in, indorsement of an instrument.

The reader is advised at this stage to refresh the memory of what is meant by 'conversion' and 'true owner' on p. 151 above, under the heading 'Conversion'.

The collecting banker   This section replaces section 82 of the 1882 Act and other enactments, and at the same time improves the position of the collecting banker relative to his common law liability of conversion. Observe that

(1) The bank must act in good faith;

(2) The bank must act without negligence;

(3) The bank must collect for a customer;

(4) The instruments may be open or crossed;

(5) The customer's account may be credited before clearance of the cheques etc. without prejudicing the bank;

(6) The instruments concerned are not only cheques but also analogous instruments, banker's drafts and Paymaster-General warrants.

Compliance with this section by the collecting banker will avoid the automatic liability for conversion arising from the collection of the proceeds of cheques etc. for someone with a defective title or no title at all. Nevertheless, note that the bank may act negligently and/or may act for a stranger and not a customer; but if he collects for the true owner he will be secure. He requires no protection against his liability for conversion where there has been no conversion. In other words section 4 is of importance only where the bank collects for someone other than the true owner.

The section is clear in intent and meaning except for the terms 'negligence' and 'customer'. The latter emerges from past litigation as simply a person having an account with a banker. Apparently the first transaction on the account is sufficient to constitute that person a customer and even if that transaction is the collection of a cheque this section 4 will apply immediately to the transactions. Even if the bank failed to take up references that a stranger should supply in opening an account, the man would still be a customer. (See below for negligence.) But the opening of the account must be with the intention of remaining a customer and not merely to facilitate the collection of one cheque.

Negligence   Whether a collecting banker acts negligently or not must be determined by the facts of the individual case. The Act does not guide us here. Section 82 (now repealed) of the Act of 1882 which section 4 of the Cheques Act replaces provided similarly that the banker must collect without negligence and numerous actions in the courts since 1882 have supplied us with interpretations of the word 'negligence' and we now have a formidable list of ways and circumstances in which bankers have in the past been considered negligent in the collection of cheques etc. The main test in most cases is whether the circumstances surrounding the transaction are sufficient to cause a reasonable business man to be put on enquiry and to cause him to delay the collection until a satisfactory explanation is forthcoming. In other words, it is not the unusual transaction itself that forms the basis of negligence but rather the failure to make the enquiry it calls for and/or the failure to obtain the satisfactory explanation.

Instances where the courts have attributed negligence to a collecting banker fall into three groups:
(1) Where the bank has failed to attend to all the necessary formalities in opening the account for the customer who, later, converts cheques etc. and uses the bank to collect the proceeds.
(2) Where the relationship between the bank's customer and the drawer or payee of the converted instrument is such as to warrant enquiry.

(3) All other cases where enquiry into the proposed collection is, according to the courts, warranted.

Group one
(a) Failure to obtain satisfactory references or failure to follow up references on opening an account. (*Harding v London Joint Stock Bank Ltd; Marfani & Co Ltd v Midland Bank Ltd* [1967] 3 All ER 967; *Lumsden & Co v London Trustee Savings Bank* [1971] Lloyds Rep 114). After all, a reference will help to establish the identity of the proposed customer and confirm any further information he gives as to his address, occupation and (in so many cases) the name and address of his employer. It is normal banking practice today to obtain this information concerning new customers and it avoids putting a cheque book in undesirable hands to the danger of the public. The practice also prevents a thief's opening a banking account in the name of the payee of cheques he has stolen so as to avoid detection or embarrassing enquiries.

(b) Failure to obtain the name of a customer's employers. (*Savory (EB) & Co v Lloyds Bank Ltd* (1932) 148 LT 291; see p. 182 below.) If a bank knows where its customer is employed (and keeps such information up to date) it should be able to avoid being used, innocently, as a party to conversion when a customer steals cheques payable to his employer and hands them to his bank for collection for his own account. (See Group two below.) It is interesting to observe in the case of *Orbit Mining & Trading Co Ltd v Westminster Bank Ltd* [1962] 3 All ER 565, that it is not the duty of the bank 'continually to keep itself up to date' as to the identity of a customer's employer.

(c) Failure to obtain the name of the employers of the husband where an account is opened for a married woman. (*Savory (EB) & Co v Lloyds Bank Ltd* (1932) 148 LT 291; see p. 182 below.) If a bank holds this information it can check any attempt to pass stolen cheques, payable to or drawn by the husband's employers, for collection and credit to the wife's account, the wife being no doubt an accomplice of the thief, the huband.

(d) Before 1981 anyone trading under a business name, i.e. a name other than his true one was asked by his ba.ik to produce a Certificate of Business Name, as registered with the Registrar of Business Names. Otherwise it was open to anyone to steal cheques payable to a certain business and get them colleçted by a bank so that the proceeds might be misused. That Registry is now closed. It is nevertheless thought that in such circumstances, now, the bank asked to accept such cheques for collection should insist on the customer's production of samples of his business note-paper and business forms that show his name as the proprietor of such a business. The position is the same if the customer is a partnership or company trading under a name other than its proper name.

Group two
(a) Collecting for the private account of a director cheques and similar documents payable to his company.
(b) Collecting for the private account of a partner cheques and similar documents payable to the partnership.
(c) Collecting for the private account of an employee cheques and similar documents payable to his employer or cheques drawn by the employer (*Savory (EB) & Co v Lloyds Bank Ltd* (1932) 148 LT 291; see p. 182, below).
(d) Collecting for a married woman's account cheques and similar documents drawn by or payable to the husband's employers (*Savory (E B) & Co v Lloyds Bank Ltd* (1932) 148 LT 291; see p. 182, below).
(e) Collecting for the private account of an agent cheques and similar documents drawn by him on his principal's account (*Morison v London County & Westminster Bank Ltd* (1914); see p. 183, below).
(f) Collecting for the private account of an agent cheques and similar documents payable to the agent but indicating that he should receive the proceeds only as agent (*Marquis of Bute v Barclays Bank Ltd* [1954] 3 All ER 365; see p. 183, below).

In each of these cases in Group two it is obvious that the circumstances are such as to facilitate the theft of cheques etc. the property of others concerned in the relationship outlined

Group three
(a) Collecting cheques etc. payable to a Limited Company for any account other than that of the company. (*London & Montrose Shipbuilding & Repairing Co Ltd v Barclays Bank Ltd* (1926) 31 Com Cas 182.) On the other hand, in *Penmount Estates Ltd v National Provincial Bank Ltd* (1945) 173 LT 344 the bank in similar circumstances succeeded. The position, consequently,

is not free from doubt, but few banks today would collect in such circumstances without a full enquiry.

(b) Collecting cheques etc. the amount of which are inconsistent with the customer's station in life or business. (*Motor Traders Guarantee Corpn v Midland Bank Ltd* [1937] 4 All ER 90; *Baker v Barclays Bank Ltd* [1955] 2 All ER 571; *Nu-Stilo Footwear Ltd v Lloyds Bank Ltd* (1956); see pp. 183 to 184, below).

(c) Collecting cheques etc. Payable to a third party in circumstances that warranted enquiry (several court cases on this issue including the *Nu-Stilo Footwear* case above).

(d) Collecting cheques etc. crossed 'account payee' for any account other than that of the payee.

The above three groups do not represent a complete inventory but nevertheless give a general picture of the pitfalls awaiting the collecting banker. The degree of care that the courts expect from him today to avoid the charge of negligence intensifies. In 1928 in the case of *Lloyds Bank Ltd v Chartered Bank of India, Australia and China* (1928) TLR 534, it was ruled that officials of banks are not expected to be amateur detectives. In 1931 in *Slingsby v Westminster Bank Ltd* [1931] 1 KB 173, the same ruling was repeated. Since then the position has appeared to change and the courts today by recent decisions seem to expect far greater care from the collecting banker, at a time too when the tempo of his work has increased far beyond that of the pre-machine era of the nineteen-twenties. A late development of the law and its attitude to the statutory protection of collecting bankers may have been witnessed in Ceylon in the case of *Bank of Ceylon v Kulatilleke* (59 Ceylon NLR 188), where it was decided that such protection does not apply to instruments that have been tampered with and bear the taint of forgery or fraudulent alteration. It is possible that this may become a precedent for our English courts, particularly so since such a view was expressed by the learned Judge (obiter) in the *Slingsby case* (*Slingsby v District Bank Ltd* [1932] 1 KB 544); in which case a banker, who collects for other than the true owner a cheque or similar instrument that has been fraudulently altered, will be without any protection against his common law liability for conversion. We must wait upon events. The position of the *paying* banker in similar circumstances has of course already been reviewed in our study of section 64 of the 1882 Act (above).

Subsection 1(b) is included in section 4 since the Bills of Exchange (Crossed Cheques) Act of 1906 is now repealed. The latter Act laid down that although a collecting banker credited his customer's account before the various items received for collecting were 'cleared', he was nevertheless collecting for a customer and that his statutory protection was not by this impaired.

Subsection 3 in the spirit of the Act designed to facilitate the abolition of indorsements provides for the collecting banker to be able to collect unindorsed or irregularly indorsed instruments without losing his statutory protection afforded by section 4. Whether this can be extended to cover unindorsed third-party cheques, etc., is not entirely free from doubt.

Bankers collecting as holders for value

(1) *Where he is the payee or indorsee of the instrument*   If the banker is the payee or indorsee then, providing the instrument is not overdue and (where he is the indorsee) providing there has been no forgery of an essential indorsement, he will have a perfect title to the instrument; he will be the true owner and consequently no question of conversion can arise. But if he is the indorsee and a prior indorsement has been forged, or if the instrument is crossed 'Not Negotiable' and possession has come through someone with no title or with a defective title then the banker will not be a holder in due course. The true owner will claim from him the instrument or the proceeds thereof. There can be no question of pleading section 4 since he collects here for himself alone. (Such an instrument could come into his hands for payment of stocks and shares, National Savings Certificates, Premium Savings Bonds, rent of offices above the bank, etc.)

(2) *Cases where he may be both holder for value and agent for collection*

(a) Where he allows the customer an absolute right to draw against the instrument before the proceeds have been cleared. It must be an *absolute* right either by specific agreement regarding one cheque or by the bank's conceding a permanent absolute right to its customer regarding all cheques he pays in for collection. (*Westminster Bank Ltd v Zang* [1966] 2 WLR 110).

(b) Where he collects for a customer an instrument over which he, the banker, has a lien. If the customer owes any obligation, debt or liability to the bank on any account or in any way then the banker has a right of lien on all of that customer's property coming into his hands in the normal course of banking business.

The right of lien will cover any cheques and other instruments paid in for collection to the extend of the lien. (Section 27(3) of the 1882 Act states that 'where the holder of a bill has a lien on it . . . he is deemed to be a holder for value to the extent of the sum for which he has a lien'.)

Until the *Zang* case, it had been thought that a banker became a holder for value when he received a cheque for collection which, being credited, reduced an existing overdraft. Since this case it is now clear that this is not so.

A collecting banker who can claim to be a holder in due course and at the same time claim the protection of section 4 is in a strong position. If his claim as a holder in due course fails he may yet claim the help of section 4 and avoid liability to the true owner. Conversely, he may collect negligently or in some other way lose the protection of section 4, yet if his claim to be a holder in due course succeeds (which it may since the question of negligence does not arise with a holder in due course) he can be unassailed by the claims of others.

Like that of the paying banker, the collecting banker's liability to the true owner lasts for six years from the date of collection of the instrument in point.

Banker collecting and paying the same cheque   Quite frequently a banker receives for collection a cheque drawn on himself by some other customer. Here the banker plays a dual role, first as collecting agent and then as paying banker. If any question of conversion arises with the cheque, then the banker must establish statutory protection to cover the two roles.

A brief summary of the important cases mentioned under this section follows.

Savory (E.B.) & Co v Lloyds Bank Ltd **(1932) 148 LT 291**
E B Savory & Co were London stockbrokers and two of their clerks, Perkins and Smith, from time to time misappropriated bearer cheques drawn by their employers payable to stock jobbers and paid them into London branches of Lloyds Bank for the credit of, in the case of Perkins, his account at the Wallington branch of that bank and in Smith's case for his wife's account at the Redhill, and later, the Weybridge branches of that bank. The branches of Lloyds Bank that conducted these accounts had not, on opening the accounts
(a) in the case of Perkins, ascertained the name of his employers and
(b) in the case of Mrs Smith, ascertained the name of her husband's employers.

The bank failed to obtain statutory protection from its common law liability for conversion since it was considered to be guilty of negligence in two respects, viz.,
(1) the branches which maintained the accounts were not possessed of information to enable the bank to keep watch on what was paid into the account so to detect any misappropriation of the employers' cheques.
(2) the London branches failed to pass on to the 'home' branch details of the cheques paid in by Perkins and Smith and cleared by the London branches on behalf of the 'home' branches.

Motor Traders Guarantee Corpn v Midland Bank Ltd [1937] 4 All ER 90
A motor trader named Turner induced Motor Traders Guarantee Corporation to hand him a cheque for £189 5s, payable to a firm of car dealers, representing that the money was due under a hire-purchase transaction. Turner misappropriated the cheque and the Midland Bank collected it for his account, not without first asking for an explanation and receiving a plausible story.

The bank failed to get statutory protection because it was considered to have acted negligently, the negligence being the collection of a sum of money large enough then to be inconsistent with Turner's business—the bank had dishonoured 35 of Turner's cheques in the previous six months.

Morison v London County and Westminster Bank Ltd [1914] 3 KB 356
Henry Abbott was authorised to draw cheques 'per pro' his employer Morison in his capacity as Manager of Morison's business. In fraud of his employer, Abbott drew 50 cheques on his employer's banking account between 1907 and 1911 which were all collected for and credited to Abbott's private account by London County & Westminster Bank. Morison sued the bank for conversion and the bank failed to invoke statutory protection since it was judged to have acted negligently by collecting cheques, without enquiry, for the private account of the agent such cheques having been drawn by him on his principal's account.

The opportunity for fraud is obviously ever present in such circumstances.

Marquis of Bute v Barclays Bank Ltd [1954] 1 QB 202 [1954] 3 All ER 365
McGaw had been the Manager of three sheep farms for the Marquis of Bute. After the termination of his employment he received three warrants totalling £546, being subsidies, payable to McGaw 'for the Marquis of Bute'. They were collected and credited to McGaw's private account without enquiry by Barclays Bank, Barnsley.

In defence, Barclays Bank advanced that:

(a) As the warrants were payable to McGaw he was the true owner notwithstanding that he was accountable for the proceeds to the Marquis.

(b) The Marquis was estopped against the bank since he knew that the warrants would be issued payable to McGaw.

(c) The bank was entitled to statutory protection if its defence in (a) failed.

The judgment declared that although the warrants were payable to McGaw, the intention of the drawer was that the Marquis should receive the money and not McGaw—the latter was merely accountable to the Marquis. Consequently conversion of the warrants had taken place and the bank was guilty of conversion. The statutory protection it claimed was lost because the court declared that the warrants bore clear evidence that McGaw was to receive the money only as an agent and elementary banking agreed that such documents cannot be credited to the agent's private account without enquiry.

Nu-Stilo Footwear Ltd v Lloyds Bank Ltd (1956) Times 19 June

Nu-Stilo Footwear employed M as its Secretary. M opened an account at Lloyds Bank in a false name of B saying he, B, was a freelance agent just commencing business. For reference he gave his real name and address and later, when Lloyd's Bank followed up the reference, he said that this man 'B' was a suitable person to be given banking facilities. Subsequently 9 cheques drawn by Nu-Stilo, most of them payable to B were collected by Lloyds Bank for 'B's' account. Since the total of these cheques was £4,855 the court ruled that they were inconsistent with B's commencing business as a freelance agent. Consequently negligence was attributed to the bank which therefore failed to get the statutory protection it claimed.

Baker v Barclays Bank Ltd [1955] 2 All ER 571

Bainbridge, a partner in a firm, trading as 'Modern Confections' misappropriated cheques payable to the firm and passed them on to a third party 'J' who successfully obtained their collection by Barclays Bank for J's account. The fraudulent partner indorsed the cheques for the firm, as he was entitled to, and J explained to his bank, Barclays, that Bainbridge was trading as Modern Confections and that J was assisting him on the financial side prior to his joining Bainbridge in partnership.

The court held that this explanation should not have been considered satisfactory, that it did not free the bank from negligence in the matter and that in consequence the bank failed to get statutory protection.

Westminster Bank Ltd v Zang [1966] 2 WLR 110

This case which went to the House of Lords was not uncomplicated but its main concern seems to have been to ascertain whether Westminster Bank Ltd collecting a cheque for the credit of an account already overdrawn was in consequence a holder for value (as well as a collecting banker); the case also brought up the collection of a cheque and payment against it before it was cleared. Briefly the facts were as follows. Tilley's Autos Ltd banked with Westminster Bank Ltd. They paid in a cheque for £1,000 drawn by Mr Zang. Before it was cleared that bank had paid cheques drawn by Tilley's Autos Ltd, paying them ostensibly against the uncleared effects. The cheque of Mr Zang was not honoured by his bankers and Westminster Bank sought to be regarded as a holder for value on the grounds that paying cheques against that uncleared cheque was in law giving value for it—in short they wanted to establish a title to the cheque for a holder in due course and thus compel the drawer (Mr Zang) to pay the cheque. Alternatively, the bank pleaded that since the cheque was collected for and reduced an overdrawn account (of Tilley's Autos) they were holders for value. This latter plea was rejected by the House of Lords. As to the former plea, the bank might have succeeded if they could have shown that they had allowed Tilley's Autos Ltd, an *absolute* right to draw against the Zang cheque before clearance (either by special arrangement regarding the Zang cheque or by showing that Tilley's Autos Ltd had a permanent absolute right to draw against all their uncleared effects at any time). However, merely to pay against uncleared effects by a unilateral decision of the bank and not by specific agreement with the customer is *not* sufficient to constitute the bank's giving value. The bank has to show, now, quite positively, that the cheques paid against the uncleared effects would have been dishonoured but for the receipt of the cheque(s) etc. for collection.

Lumsden & Co v London Trustee Savings Bank ((1971) Lloyds Rep 114)

Here was a case of a collecting banker found guilty of conversion without the protection of section 4, Cheques Act 1957 in its failure to obtain a satisfactory introductory reference relating to a new customer. The latter in this case was a stranger who offered the name of 'Dr Blake' as a referee. The latter replied favourably to the bank but did not supply the name of his own bankers so that the London Trustee Savings Bank could check that he was a suitable person to act as referee. The rules of that bank clearly stated that this was absolutely essential in like circumstances but in this case the bank decided to 'skip' it, having been informed that Dr Blake had recently arrived in the UK from Australia probably without UK bankers. Cheques drawn by Lumsden & Co were misappropriated and passed through the defendant bank, the proceeds being quickly withdrawn. The whole story of the thief turned out to be a tissue of lies which would have been revealed, said the court, if the defendant bank had been more diligent, demanding at least the sight of the 'Dr Blake' with his passport.

5.   Application of certain provisions of Bills of Exchange Act 1882, to instruments not being bills of exchange
The provisions of the Bills of Exchange Act 1882, relating to crossed cheques shall, so far as applicable, have effect in relation to instruments (other than cheques) to which the last foregoing section applies as they have effect in relation to cheques.

This section extends the provision of sections 76 to 81 of the 1882 Act (which sections refer only to 'cheques') to all those documents that do the work of a cheque yet fail to comply with its legal definition. Such documents are listed in section 4 above. The main effect of section 5 is that the protection of sections 79 and 80 of the 1882 Act protecting the banker paying cheques is extended to analogous instruments, banker's drafts, etc. drawn on him. (Before the Chques Act 1957, the protection of these sections was extended to cover the banker by virtue of other enactments, now repealed).

6.   Construction, saving and repeal
(1) This Act shall be construed as one with the Bills of Exchange Act 1882.

(2) The foregoing provisions of this Act do not make negotiable any instrument which, apart from them, is not negotiable.

(3) The enactments mentioned in the first and second columns of the Schedule to this Act are hereby repealed to the extent specified in the third column of that Schedule.

Subsection 2 here appears a simple and reasonable statement. The same point was expressed by section 17 of the Revenue Act, 1883 (repealed—see below). Whilst that was operative it was generally interpreted as meaning that any instrument considered non-*transferable* was not made transferable by virtue of section 17 of the Revenue Act. In other words, the word 'negotiable' was given its wider meaning of 'transferable'. If the same interpretation can be given to section 6 here then we must say that this Act does not make transferable any instrument that is not transferable. In consequence bankers must collect such instruments only for the account of the payee and paying bankers must identify the payee if payment is made in cash or, if payment is made through the Clearings, ensure that the instrument bears no evidence of transfer. See section 81 of the 1882 Act above.

7. Provisions as to Northern Ireland

8. Short title and commencement

These sections are of little interest to bankers or the general student of negotiable instruments.

SCHEDULE

ENACTMENTS REPEALED

Session and Chapter	*Short Title*	*Extent of Repeal*
45 & 46 Vict. c. 61	The Bills of Exchange Act 1882	Section 82
46 & 47 Vict. c. 55	The Revenue Act 1883	Section 17
6 Edw. 7 c, 17	The Bills of Exchange (Crossed Cheques) Act 1906	The whole Act
22 & 23 Geo. 5 c. 44	The Bills of Exchange Act (1882) Amendment Act 1932	The whole Act

Banker's drafts A banker's draft is a draft drawn payable to order by a bank as drawer on the same bank as drawee. It is of no matter whether the draft is payable at Head Office or any office of the same bank. In all cases it is tantamount to the bank drawing on itself since all branches of the same bank are treated as one entity for this purpose.

A banker's draft is not strictly a legal cheque since drawer and drawee are the same person. However, by virtue of the Cheques Act 1957 the protection of bankers paying and collecting such instruments is as with valid cheques.

Since the drawer of a banker's draft is a bank then there is no fear of dishonour through lack of funds and these instruments are in popular demand for use in business transactions where cash or its near equivalent is needed (e.g. property purchases). Dishonour of a banker's draft however is not impossible since no bank would pay against one if they had reliable knowledge that it was in wrong hands.

A draft drawn by one bank on another bank is of course a valid bill. Such drawings arise where payment is required in cash in a certain town where the drawer bank has no branch.

N.B.—A banker's draft must not be drawn payable to bearer. Section 5(2) of the 1882 Act provides that where drawer and drawee are the same person, the bill may be treated as a promissory note. Consequently where the same person is a bank the instrument could be treated as a *bank note*. By the Bank Charter Act 1844, bank notes may be issued now only by the Bank of England. Consequently, banks drawing banker's drafts must draw them to order.

Conditional orders   Section 3 of the 1882 Act states that a valid bill is an *unconditional* order in writing etc., etc. Consequently an order to a banker to pay a sum of money to a named payee provided a receipt on the document itself is duly completed is an order with a condition and not therefore a valid bill of exchange or valid cheque. This instrument is known as a conditional order. It is outside the direct application of the Act of 1882 but the Cheques Act in sections 1 and 4 speaks of 'any document issued by a customer . . . which, though not a bill of exchange, is intended to enable a person to obtain payment . . . of the sum mentioned in the document'. Consequently, it would appear that bankers paying or collecting such instruments would have the same protection as though they were cheques. However, section 6(2) above says the provisions of this Act do not make an instrument negotiable if elsewhere it is considered not negotiable. And the word 'negotiable' here may mean 'transferable'. So to be really safe in handling these documents it may be necessary to collect only for the account of the payee and to pay in cash on identification or through the Clearings providing there is no evidence of transfer on the document (e.g. the endorsement of some other person in addition to the receipt of the payee).

The use of the conditional order being a receipt for completion has greatly fallen off since 1957 and drawers of such instruments have largely reverted to using cheques, relying on section 3 of the Cheques Act 1957, which states that the paid cheque is evidence of receipt. In any case, if the conditional order is still considered as a non-transferable instrument, then bankers must strongly discourage their use in view of the Resolution of the London Clearing bankers—see section 81 of the 1882 Act.

Part 4
Miscellaneous enactments

Miscellaneous enactments

Stamp Act 1853

19. Drafts on bankers payable to order on demand, and indorsed by payees, shall be sufficient authority for payment, etc. Any draft or order drawn upon a banker for a sum of money payable to order on demand, which shall, when presented for payment, purport to be indorsed by the person to whom the same shall be drawn payable, shall be a sufficient authority to such banker to pay the amount of such draft or order to the bearer thereof; and it shall not be incumbent on such banker to prove that such indorsement, or any subsequent indorsement, was made by or under the direction or authority of the person to whom the said draft or order was or is made payable either by the drawer or any indorser thereof.

Bills of Exchange (Time of Noting) Act 1917

1. Time of noting. In subsection (4) of section fifty-one of the Bills of Exchange Act 1882 (which relates to the time of noting a dishonoured bill), the words 'it must be noted on the day of its dishonour' shall be repealed, and the following words shall be substituted therefor, namely, 'it may be noted on the day of its dishonour and must be noted not later than the next succeeding business day'.

2. Short title and construction. This Act may be cited as the Bills of Exchange (Time of Noting) Act 1917.

Post Office Act 1953

21. Special provisions as to postal orders. . . . (3) Any person acting as a banker . . . who in collecting in that capacity for any principal, has received payment . . . in respect of any postal order, or of any document purporting to be a postal order, shall not incur liability to anyone except that principal by reason of having received the payment . . . or having held or presented the order or document for payment. . .

As the Post Office is the authority paying postal orders, the question of the paying banker does not arise. Bankers collect millions of postal orders, however, and this Act provides protection so long as they merely collect for a principal. This protection is, however, very theoretical since postal orders are invariably credited as cash before collection is made and this automatically places a collecting banker outside the scope of this Act.

Part 5

Highlights of the Legislation
Banks and Negotiable Instruments
Building Societies
Past Examination Questions
Bankers Cards and Credit Cards

Chapter 1
Highlights of the legislation

With the almost total disappearance of the trade bill from domestic usage (it now being equated with foreign trade) the parts of the legislation of 1882 and the Cheques Act which concern most of us are those sections concerning cheques and like documents. The following observations pin-point our involvements as we pay our way and receive cheques in the course of our normal life.

Holder in due course
Too much is made of the protection afforded by crossing a cheque. That action merely hinders a thief. It will not save one from the claims of a holder in due course. The public speak of 'cancelling' a cheque by countermand of payment made to the drawee bank. This is nonsense. One cannot 'cancel' one's liability as a party to a cheque merely by instructing one's bankers not to pay it. A holder in due course of a cheque, though dishonoured by the drawee bank, may still invoke the law and enforce payment against the drawer himself.

Duty of the paying banker to pay his customer's cheques
If no legal bar exists and adequate funds are available in the customer's account, the drawee bank must pay its customer's cheque. If it is presented in the Clearing then normally the drawee bank has until the close of business that day to pay it or dishonour it. But if the cheque is uncrossed and presented for cash at the bank counter, the bank must pay or dishonour immediately. The fact that the presenter is a stranger, the fact that the cheque is for a substantial sum, these are irrelevant; the decision to pay or not must be made immediately. The drawee bank is fully covered if it complies with sections 59 or 60 of the 1882 Act. There are reports of bank cashiers asking for proof of identity of the payee notwithstanding that the presenter may not be the payee—the cheque

is fully transferable, no doubt with endorsement. Cheques are payable on demand and not on proof of identity. Unwarranted delay in making the payment over the counter will one day see a bank defending an action for breach of contract.

Material alteration
It is not illegal to draw a cheque in pencil or to leave large gaps in writing the amount in words. The public are well aware of the danger of fraudulent alteration and they no doubt take care in drawing cheques, largely because they fear that the results may be to their loss, notwithstanding that they know nothing of the celebrated *MacMillan* case. Section 64 of the 1882 Act makes this clear. It is necessary to point out, though, that an 'apparent' alteration against the forged initials of the drawer is of no concern to the drawer of the cheque and any loss sustained by such criminal act must be that of the drawee bank if it pays such a cheque. This is a risk that a drawee bank must inevitably face. Initials are so easy to forge on a cheque when it already bears the full signature of the drawer.

Stale cheques, overdue cheques etc.
It is well known that a cheque bearing a date six months or more prior to its date of presentation to the drawee bank for payment will be dishonoured as 'stale'. Though the drawer of his cheque is liable on his signature for six years, his bank rightly thinks it in his own interest to have second thoughts as to payment and consequently refuses payment. This is no breach of contract since it is the normal course of business. In practice, the holder of the cheque would request the drawer to alter the date or alternatively issue a duplicate, and this request would be hard to refuse since, as we have seen, the drawer is liable on his signature for six years. Even if such a cheque be deemed 'overdue' within the meaning of the Act of 1882, this will not discharge the drawer from his liability; such merely affects the possibility of a transferee being a holder in due course (section 29 of the 1882 Act).

Crossings of cheques: the paying banker
He has a duty to his customer and a duty to himself. His duty is to pay the cheque in accordance with the crossing. If it be crossed to

two bankers then he should refuse to pay it if he feels that there might have been conversion of the cheque, which would involve him, no doubt, in a court action. Likewise, any crossed cheque should not be paid in cash at the counter but paid to a bank presenting it (normally) through the Clearing. But surely it is obvious that if the paying bank is quite satisfied that there has been no conversion of the cheque, the cheque should be paid. In addition, since the chances of theft etc. of the cheque are remote, a sensible attitude might be adopted in the case of cheques for very trifling amounts. As an old bankman once said, 'we are here to pay cheques of our customers and not to dishonour them at the slightest excuse'. The sight of a bank cashier, insisting that the drawer-customer at the counter should cancel the crossing of his cheque before cashing it, the cheque bearing a printed crossing and the customer so well known to the cashier, is laughable.

The collecting banker
Before 1957 (the Cheques Act) the collecting banker got his statutory protection only with crossed cheques and his paying-in slips bore the printed request that the customer should cross all cheques before paying them in for collection. (The fact that such printed request still appears in the case of some banks is somewhat puzzling.) The Cheques Act extended the statutory protection to all cheques and like instruments whether open or crossed. Thus crossings on the whole are much less important to the collecting banker. Naturally, he must respect the 'Account-payee' crossing and not accept such cheques unless there be a satisfactory explanation as to why it cannot go to the banking account of the named payee. If such a cheque is for a trifling sum, then a collecting banker who refuses to collect the cheque with or without a reasonable explanation, is being thoroughly unhelpful to his customer. Regretfully this is taking place as though collecting such a cheque is a criminal act.

Cheques bearing the 'not negotiable' crossing are, as far as the collecting banker is concerned, collecting the cheque for his customer, merely crossed cheques with a general crossing. One hears repeatedly of cashiers refusing to accept such cheques for collection unless they be placed to the account of the payee. This causes inconvenience to the customer and shows marked ignorance of the business of banking. We have already found out on earlier pages that such words do *not* prohibit transfer, and have importance only to transferees who may have to prove that they be holders in due course. Thus, the only time when a collecting banker might consider the importance of such words must be when he gives value for the cheque himself before collection, by, for example, allowing payments against it before clearance.

Chapter 2
Banks and negotiable instruments

Cheques
Banks pay cheques in their millions each year. Few are negotiable since they are not payable to bearer or, being payable to order, are not indorsed in blank. Cheques are issued to the payee and in almost every case, paid by the payee into his bank account. Thus only where the payee has no bank account do we find that the cheque becomes a negotiable instrument, since he indorses it in blank and cashes it with a shopkeeper or like tradesman.

Bank Notes
In England, the Bank of England has the monopoly of bank-note issue. Such notes are legal tender. People go shopping with them. If they need more than they get in wage packets they get them by cashing a cheque at their bankers. Such banks are legally bound to repay their deposits in legal tender and that means of course the notes of the Bank of England. They are payable to bearer and fully negotiable. We cannot cross them 'not negotiable' since that would render the note worthless. Banks keep such quantity in their safes as they feel they need to satisfy normal withdrawals of deposits. They have strong rooms for their safe-keeping. Even the banking halls of our great banks look like fortresses as we do our banking business there.

Treasury bills
These are receipts for cash lent to the Government. They incorporate a promies to repay the loan in (usually) 91 days. Thus they are promissory notes rather than bills. Each week the Bank of England acting for the Treasury invites offers of cash, much of which will be used to repay bills maturing that week. Our large commercial banks like to hold them as a good lock-up of funds. They are payable to 'bearer' and fully negotiable. Any bank which finds

itself short of cash can sell these bills in the Discount Market in minutes. Banks do not normally apply to the Bank of England but prefer the Discount Houses to take them up on issue and to re-sell to the commercial banks a few days later.

Trade bills

Commercial banks discount such bills (which arise mainly through foreign trade) and become holders in due course if they fulfil the requirements of section 29 of the 1882 Act. They do not discount bills for strangers unless they are introduced by a foreign bank under a Documentary Letter of Credit. If such bills of exchange bear the signature of a London Acceptance House (Merchant Bank) then the payment of the bill at maturity is assured.

The only other way in which they become involved with bills is when they pay their customers' acceptances domiciled with the bank. It is quite normal for the acceptor to add to his signature 'Payable at the XY Bank Warmington-on-Sea'. The bank has no statutory protection if it fails to make payment in due course as it certainly has with cheques. Banks like to take an indemnity from their customers against this risk.

Bearer bonds

Foreign governments and some foreign companies issue bonds as acknowledgements of money lent to them. Banks hold them usually as custodians for their customers. Attached to the bonds are sheets of coupons numbered and dated ahead. When interest is due for collection, the banks clip off the relative coupon (negotiable) and present them to the paying agent for receipt of the money and credit to the customer's account.

American-type share certificate

These have already been reviewed and classified as quasi negotiable. Once endorsed in blank by the shareholder (stockholder) they can be transferred by simple delivery. They are held by banks normally situated in London who present them to the paying agent when interest or dividend is due for collection. The paying agent stamps them to signify that the money has been paid and back they go to the bank for safe keeping until the next payment is due.

Chapter 3
Building societies and other deposit-taking institutions

In the last two or three decades we have witnessed a rapid expansion of societies, companies and other institutions seeking the spare money of the public. A common feature is the offer of attractive rates of interest that mostly (but not always) compare favourably with those of the commercial banks. Except where the amount is considerable, the deposits are withdrawable in cash on demand and it is not an unimportant factor that their offices are open on Saturday mornings. The building societies have been singled out by the banks for criticism on the grounds of unfair competition. Certainly the spread of building societies' branch offices along the high street of every town is very noticeable as is also the extent of their advertising. Since all their monies received from their 'investors' is paid immediately into the bank accounts of the societies, the charge of stealing away money from the banks is not easily understood.

What is patently obvious however is that these institutions are now receiving thousands of cheques daily for the credit of deposit accounts, the cheques then being handed to commercial banks for collection to the account of the society. Thus the risk of innocent involvement in conversion must have grown enormously. The Building Societies Association report that so far the problem or danger of such involvement has been in practice slight and that no-one has yet pressed for the statutory protection that banks enjoy under section 4 of The Cheques Act. But they are well aware of the danger and have taken certain measures to minimise the risk. For example, societies have been warned by their Association that cheques payable to companies should not be accepted for the credit of an individual person's account without making considerable enquiries. Even if he should pay in a cheque payable to a third party, most societies are conscious of the danger—those who merely insist that the cheque bear the endorsement of the third-party payee do themselves little good since that can so easily be supplied by forgery. It appears obvious that these societies must

protect themselves by insisting on new depositors (investors) sup-
plying references, his place of employment (if any), etc. just as
commercial banks must do to avoid the charge of negligence under
section 4 of the Cheques Act.

The fact that building societies do not normally supply current
account facilities must explain the near-freedom so far from
involvements in conversion attempts. Large sums deposited by
cheque with a society followed by a rapid attempt to withdraw the
money would appear to arouse suspicions much more than with a
commercial bank current account.

We must await developments. If experience shows the need for
statutory protection on the lines of section 4 of the Cheques Act, it
would seem unfair to deny them of this.

Obviously, where any deposit-taking institution complies with
the necessary requirements and becomes recognised as a 'bank',
then the normal protection is available.

Chapter 4

Past examination questions of The Law Society and the Institute of Bankers

The Law Society

Question 1

(a) Simon drew an uncrossed cheque for £400 in favour of John in payment for a motor car. The cheque was stolen from John by a thief who forged an endorsement by John in favour of Richard in payment for a diamond ring. Richard did not hand over the ring until he and the thief together had been to the bank on which the cheque was drawn and payment had been made by the bank to Richard. Advise John.

(b) How would it affect your advice if Simon had not been involved? Instead, the theft had been of John's cheque book and the forgery had been of John's signature to his own cheque.

August 1976

Answer 1

(a) Richard had no title to the cheque. The special indorsement to him was a forgery and therefore no title passed to him. John can enforce his claim against Richard.

John obviously has a right of action against the thief for what it is worth.

The paying banker will be deemed to have paid the cheque in due course notwithstanding the forgery of the indorsement providing it has complied with section 60 of the 1882 Act.

(b) If the cheque had been a forgery of John's drawing then of course John is completely free from liability. His bank cannot debit his account. Richard is liable to refund the money to the drawee bank unless he can show he has relied upon the transaction and has materially changed his position on the strength of it.

Question 2

Husband and wife opened a joint bank account on terms that

cheques drawn on the account should require both their signatures. The wife has withdrawn £1,500 by forging the husband's signature to cheques. Advise the bank in circumstances where the husband is threatening an action for a declaration that the account is wrongly debited.

Would it affect your advice if the husband had discovered the forgeries 12 months ago but had kept quiet to avoid publicity until now in circumstances where his wife has just died?

February 1977

Answer 2
The bank has no authority to debit the joint account in view of the forgery of one of the signatures. There is some doubt however as to the ability of the husband to sue the bank since the plaintiffs would have to be both himself and the forger-wife; the latter could hardly bring an action of this kind when she has been the reason for the bank's error.

If the husband had been aware of the forgeries and kept silent then he is obviously estopped from denying the signature later. See section 24 for estoppel.

Question 3
Mrs Brown made out a crossed cheque for ten pounds in favour of her grocer, 'Mr Riche'; but left a space between the printed word 'Pay' and the written words 'ten pounds'. The grocer's assistant, Richardson, takes the cheque from the till. By skilful forgery, he alters the name of the payee from Riche to Richardson and inserts the words 'one hundred and' before the words 'ten pounds' and likewise alters the figures of the cheque. He then collects payment on the cheque. Is Mrs Brown's bank entitled to debit her account and, if so, by what sum?　*August 1977*

Answer 3
This is the *MacMillan* case again. See section 64 of the 1882 Act.

Since it appears that the alteration of the amount was facilitated by the negligence of the drawer in drawing the cheque, the drawer will be liable for the swollen sum.

Question 4
To what extent (if at all) is the paying bank entitled to debit the account of the customer if, in the absence of any negligence on the part of the customer or the bank, it pays under:

(a) a forged signature of the customer;
(b) a forged endorsement of the cheque drawn by the customer; and
(c) a forged alteration of the amount of the cheque as drawn by the customer from £10 to £110?   *February 1978*

Answer 4

(a) The forgery of the drawer's signature means that the bank has no mandate. The only exception here is based on the doctrine of estoppel. See question 2 above.

(b) The bank paying a cheque bearing a forged endorsement can look to statutory protection against its common law conversion. Open cheques—section 60 of the 1882 Act; crossed cheques—section 80 of the same Act.

(c) The *MacMillan* case again. See section 64 of the 1882 Act. If the alteration (equivalent to forgery) is non-apparent and has been facilitated by the drawer's negligent drawing of the cheque then the drawer must stand the loss. If the alteration is obvious and apparent with a forgery of the drawer's signature (or initials) against the alteration then of course the drawer is not liable to one penny.

Question 5

A cheque for £5,000 crossed '& Co' drawn on the Beta Bank in favour of a firm of solicitors is stolen by the firm's cashier who forges the firm's indorsement in favour of his wife. She hands the cheque to the Alpha Bank, asking for an account to be opened in her name and explaining that the cheque is in respect of the proceeds of the sale of property on her behalf. Collection is duly made, and she withdraws the full amount and absconds. State with your reasons whether the Alpha and Beta Banks are liable to the solicitors in respect of this loss.   *August 1978*

Answer 5

The Alpha Bank. This is the collecting banker and it is guilty of conversion at common law. It must look to section 4 of the Cheque Act 1957 for protection. It can lose this if it is considered to have acted negligently. Was it put on enquiry when it saw the actual cheque? No. Solicitors are known to pass on cheques on which they are the payee to clients when the monies have been received by them for the client. The only doubt here is the opening of the account itself. Was a proper introduction obtained? Did the bank get details of the husband's occupation and name of his employers? If it failed to get the latter then it appears that the transaction was facilitated by the omission since a cheque for such a large amount payable to the husband's employers is surely sufficient to put the bank upon enquiry. See the *Savory Case* under section 4 of the Cheques Act.

Question 6
Colin, a cashier employed by a firm of solicitors made our a cheque for £800 in favour of P Parkinson. A partner of the firm signed the cheque as drawer. He made no enquiry as to the payee because P Parkinson was the name of a regular client.

In fact, no money was owed to P Parkinson, and Colin forged P Parkinson's indorsement on the cheque in favour of Dolly to whom he owned £800.

Dolly obtained payment on the cheque from the solicitors' bankers. Colin appears not to have returned from a holiday in the South of France and his whereabouts are unknown.

Advise Dolly whether she may retain the £800.

February 1979

Answer 6
See section 7 of the 1882 Act.

This is not a case of a non-existing payee since the partner knew of the existence of such a person, a client.

Neither would it appear to be a case of a fictitious payee since the drawer (partner) obviously (thinking that money was owing to the payee) intended payment to him. Thus the cheque is *not* payable to bearer. Dolly's title to the cheque as transferee must fall since the special indorsement to her was a forgery and that indorsement was essential for delivery. Dolly must refund.

Typical examination questions

Question 1
X draws a crossed cheque in favour of Y to pay for goods received and sends it to Y. As Y intends to pass on the cheque to his wholesaler, he endorses it but thereafter loses it in the street. Z picks it up and persuades P, a publican, to cash it for him. The cheque is duly cleared through P's bank and paid by X's bank.

Explain the legal position of X, Y, Z and P.

Would it make any difference if either X or Y had written the words 'not negotiable' inside the crossing?   *April 1973*

Answer 1

The position of X. He has patently discharged his own liability since the payee received the cheque. The point is emphasised in section 80 of the 1882 Act as follows

> if the cheque has come into the hands of the payee the drawer shall be entitled to the same rights . . . as if payment had been made to the true owner thereof.

The position of Y. He obviously has a right to sue Z the thief by finding. His right of action against the publican P will depend on whether P has complied with section 29 and established himself as a holder in due course. If he has done so then action against P would appear fruitless.

The position of Z. He is guilty of theft and fraud and is liable to be prosecuted by the police. He may still be the defendant in a civil case for conversion if Y thinks it worth while to bring the action.

The position of P. As mentioned above, if he can comply with section 29 he holds the cheque and all the monies due under the cheque as the true owner.

Not negotiable crossing. This would have destroyed P. His title would be as defective as that of Z, viz non-existing.

This question has been set many times in similar words. The author had such an experience himself when a publican asked for advice. Too many banking students get involved with crossings (which have no bearing whatsoever on the matter) and write bitter attacks on bar-tenders who should be more careful and so on. The question is a simple test of the examinee's understanding of negotiability.

Question 2

(a) With regard to bills of exchange, what is meant by:
    (i) a general acceptance;
    (ii) a qualified acceptance?

(b) A, the holder of a bill of exchange for £1,000 drawn by X, payable 4 months after date to Y (who has indorsed it), presents it to the drawee, Z, for acceptance. Advise A in the following events:
    (i) Z signs and returns the bill marked 'Accepted payable at Barset Bank Ltd, Barchester'.

(ii) Z signs and returns the bill marked 'Accepted payable for £500 only'.   *April 1974*

Answer 2
This can be found very clearly in sections 17, 19 and 44. Note the right to accept partial acceptance and still preserve rights against prior parties by normal notice to them of what had happened.

Question 3
Consider the legal implications when customers wish to pay in at a branch of North Bank Ltd for credit of their respective private accounts the following cheques:

(a) in the case of Tom, a cheque drawn by him in his own favour as attorney for Lord X;

(b) in the case of Dick, a cheque payable to Simon Snooks which, he says, is the 'nom-de-plume' under which he writes articles for magazines;

(c) in the case of Harry, a cheque payable to him already crossed in ink 'South Bank Ltd'.   *September 1974*

Answer 3
This of course involves a collecting banker, the risk of possible conversion, and what he must do in order not to lose the statutory protection of section 4 of the Cheques Act 1957.

(a) *Tom as attorney for Lord X.* See *Morison v London County & Westminster Bank* (1914) and *Midland Bank Ltd v Reckitt* [1933] AC 1.

(b) *In the case of Dick.* A cheque is freely transferable. Many people, particularly small shopkeepers constantly pay in third-party cheques for collection with their takings. It is very doubtful if the bank is put on enquiry at all. If it did ask for an explanation, the one it got is satisfactory, even though the cheque be crossed 'Account payee'.

(c) *In the case of Harry.* When the North Bank Ltd slam their crossing stamp on the cheque it will be crossed to two bankers. The drawee banker will dishonour it if it wants to keep its statutory protection under section 80 of the 1882 Act. But the collecting banker North Bank Ltd is not involved.

Question 4
Consider the legal implications for the South Bank in each of the following situations:

(a) it has inadvertently paid a 'stopped' cheque;

(b) it has cashed an open cheque five minutes after closing time, and next morning the drawer countermands payment;

(c) it has paid a crossed cheque on which the payee's indorsement has been forged;

(d) it has paid a bill of exchange domiciled with it on which the payee's indorsement has been forged.   *September 1975*

Answer 4
Revocation of the banker's authority to pay must be obeyed. The bank here must not debit the account of the drawer but it has by subrogation the rights to claim any goods involved and to sue anyone that the drawer might have sued had he paid the amount involved himself.

(b) If the person who received payment was in the bank office before closing time then the bank is no doubt clear. Otherwise such payment is not in the normal course of business and the bank would be liable if payment was not made to the holder. See section 60 of the 1882 Act.

(c) If the true owner has not received the money due under the cheque then the paying banker would be liable to him only where he had failed to pay in accordance with the crossing (e.g. payment in cash at the counter). Section 80 of the 1882 Act.

(d) If there has been conversion then the paying banker is not protected. His protection is with cheques and like instruments but not with a domiciled bill.

Question 5
Discuss the legal position of the ABC Bank in the following situations:

(a) It has paid a cheque for £80 to the debit of E's account, but the cheque was in fact drawn by E for £8 and subsequently the amount was fraudulently increased.

(b) It has inadvertently dishonoured a cheque drawn by F, who runs a small engineering business. The cheque was payable to the Gas Board, having been sent in response to a final demand. In consequence, the Gas Board cut off the supply and F loses a considerable amount of business.

Would the answer be different if F was a private housholder whose supply was cut off?   *September 1976*

Answer 5
(a) This is the *MacMillan* case. See section 64 of the 1882 Act. Though there is no authority to charge the account for more than

the original sum of £8 (in fact if the alteration is apparent the drawer is completely discharged) we know that if the alteration was facilitated by the drawer's lack of care in drawing the cheque, he will have to stand the full £80. The ease of this particular altera-tion will make it difficult to lay the blame at the door of the drawer. But no doubt the bank might try. The amount is trivial and hardly likely to get into the High Court.

(b) The paying banker is contractually bound to pay its cus-tomer's cheques providing there is no legal bar and the mandate is clear. If it is guilty of a breach here then it must face damages claimed in losing the business. The situation with the private householder is obviously different. He would have difficulty in proving financial loss.

Question 6

(a) James and John carry on a business in partnership. In the last few days James has properly indorsed a number of cheques pay-able to the partnership and cashed them at the local casino where he has been gambling heavily. The cheques are now lodged by the casino at the South Bank for the credit of its account there.

(b) Simon, another customer of the South Bank, seeks to pay in for the credit of his account a Paymaster General warrant for £200 made payable to Peter. He explains that Peter is a friend who has no bank account of his own.

Consider whether the bank should collect the cheques and the warrant.   *September 1976*

Answer 6

(a) This is based on *Baker v Barclays Bank Ltd* [1955] 2 All ER 571 where it was held that the other partner could sue in conver-sion for his wrongful exclusion from the joint property, and the collecting bank being negligent loses its statutory protection and is liable. The casino might try to prove its title as holder in due course but that is another question. They might find difficulty since there would appear to be an obvious misapplication of partnership property.

(b) There are no suspicious circumstances here. The warrant is freely transferable but if it should be crossed 'A/c Payee' the bank might rightly object.

Question 7

Advise the Omega Bank in the following situations:

(a) it has cashed over the counter a cheque drawn on it by X on which the original crossing has been removed;

(b) 25 cheques each for £30 issued by Y to a gaming club and backed by his cheque card are presented for payment when Y's account is already overdrawn up to its authorised limit of £100;

(c) a stranger telephoned to say that he is the payee of a cheque for £500 drawn on the bank by Z and that this cheque was stolen the previous night by a burglar. The next morning this cheque is presented for payment, and the bank has just ascertained that Z (a wealthy customer) is away on a sailing holiday for several weeks.

April 1977

Answer 7

(a) Of course if the crossing has been 'removed' by cancellation by the drawer and he has signed the alteration then no harm is done. If however the crossing has been fraudulently removed so as to allow anonymous cashing at the counter then the bank will not be liable to the true owner for any loss he may have sustained. Section 79 refers.

(b) The bank is liable to pay one of the cheques and can dishonour the others.

(c) Strictly speaking, only the drawer can countermand payment of his cheque. However, the bank here cannot stick strictly to the letter of the law when there may be good grounds for believing the cheque to be in wrong hands. The cheque should be dishonoured with some answer like 'Information received that this cheque may have got into wrong hands and payment is postponed pending confirmation'.

Question 8

Codd visits the Dogger Bank with his friend, who is posing as Bloater, a famous television personality, whom he closely resembles. Codd asks to open a current account, offering 'Bloater' as a referee. Thereupon 'Bloater' gives a favourable reference in respect of Codd, which the bank accepts without further inquiry. Codd then pays in a cheque for a large amount and, after it has been cleared, he withdraws almost all the proceeds. The true owner of this cheque now claims its value from the bank, and Codd cannot be found. Advise the bank.

Would you change your advice if in fact the bank had allowed Codd to draw against the cheque whilst still uncleared, and payment of it was stopped by the drawer?   *April 1978*

Answer 8

The bank here is guilty of conversion and must look to section 4 of the Cheques Act 1957 for protection. That section requires the bank to have acted without negligence and one example of negligence within the meaning of that section is the omission to obtain à satisfactory reference when an account is opened for a new customer. The acceptance of a stranger as a referee without ascertaining whether the latter is suitable to act as such is certainly negligence no matter whom the stranger resembles; indeed we cannot conclude that all television personalities are ipso facto suitable as referees.

Where a collecting banker fails to obtain the protection of section 4 of the Cheques Act he may yet escape the consequences of his act if he can show that he 'bought' the cheque, i.e. gave value for it so as to establish himself as a holder in due course in accordance with section 29 of the 1882 Act. That section does not require a transferee to act without negligence but rather to act in good faith which surely could be presumed in favour of an English Bank. It is well established that allowing payment against uncleared cheques is the equivalent of giving value.

Question 9

A draws a bill of exchange on B payable to C. The bill is in proper form and falls due three months after date. B accepts the bill and A then sends it to C, who indorses it and hands it to X in settlement of a debt.

Outline the respective promises or engagements of A, B and C as regards the bill.

Can any of them, when signing the bill, add 'sans recours' and, if so, what effect would these words have?   *April 1979*

Answer 9

The drawer 'A'. See section 55 of the 1882 Act.

The payee 'C'. See section 55 of the 1882 Act. The payee here is an indorser.

The acceptor 'B'. See section 54 of the 1882 Act.

'Sans recours'—see section 16 of the 1882 Act.

Chapter 5
Bankers cards and credit cards

Not many years ago an English commercial bank was forecasting in its advertisements that the UK was moving slowly but surely into a cashless society. This caused much merriment in certain quarters at the time but today with the wide use of 'cards' one wonders if that advertisement was after all not far from the truth, though no-one is seriously suggesting that we shall one day buy our evening newspapers in the street with a 'card'.

These cards were an American invention and were in popular use long before an English Bank took the plunge and introduced the system on a large scale in the UK. And thus, with their general use here it is not out of place to consider what effect they are having on the use of negotiable instruments as a means of payment.

Firstly, they have not reduced the number of cheques drawn by the public; rather the contrary. The number of cheques that make their way through the Bankers Clearing House is still increasing year after year. In fact it is partly through the use of these cards that the cheque book has become so popular with all classes of society. The bankers card that guarantees the payment by the drawee bank of the holder's cheques up to a given figure, say £50 a cheque, has made shopping by cheque book a normal part of our life. In addition, it is common knowledge that a bank current account, once the privilege of the well-to-do, has spread to all sections of society. We may be moving towards a cashless society but there is no sign yet of the cheque book becoming a museum piece. This does not rule out, though, the further development of the computer terminal and other pieces of modern wizardry that appears to be taking over so much of the work that was once accomplished by man, paper and ink.

Bills of exchange, so popular when Chalmers was drafting the Act of 1882, are now relegated to the field of foreign trade. The cheque, once so often used as a transferable type of money, is almost without exception used today simply as an authority for the banking system to transfer items between the current accounts of the payee and the drawer. Since such a transfer is today no longer a manual operation but a mere 'flash' among the computers, the operation can easily be performed without the use of a piece of paper, a cheque. All of us can authorise our banks to accept direct debits initiated by our creditors from time to time. We can order goods and services by telephone and by quoting a personal number the payment is effected so rapidly by the flash among the computers. Inside banking offices and also fixed into the outside wall thereof are pieces of machinery that enable us to withdraw cash without the use of a cheque or any other piece of paper.

If we can quote a number that links us to the computer into a telephone then we can quote a number to a check-out supermarket assistant in exactly the same way. As our purchases are being put into our shopping bags the money for their purchase is being removed from our current account to that of the supermarket company. With the coming of cable television we can now see the day coming when without lifting our bodies from our easy chairs we can accomplish all of our private financial transactions since the 'cable' will be our link to the computers. Common law conversion by the theft or misuse of cheques and bills of exchange is now seen as the dishonest use of the credit card of the victim. Forgery on a bill (or cheque) is being replaced with forgery of the signature of a holder of a credit card.

Bankers cards

Once the new current-account customer has won the approval of his bank he may be given a 'bankers card' that bears a specimen of his signature and acts as a guarantee of his bank to anyone who accepts cheques of the card holder that such cheques will be paid for relatively small sums (say £50 or less). Banks that provide such 'cards' are at risk since a thief who steals both cheque book and card will not have much difficulty in forging the relevant signature to a cheque and making purchases here there and everywhere. The thief will be able to cash the cheques with most banks too. Such losses must fall on the drawee bank since the cheque will bear a forged drawer's signature which is of course wholly inoperative under section 24 of the 1882 Act, unless the bank can show without any doubt that the card holder deliberately refrained from advising the theft of the 'card' to the bank concerned.

It is not appropriate in this book to consider the ways in which the card has been misused by its owner with gay abandon, spreading his cheques among the community and leaving a sizeable unsecured overdraft in his wake.

The main advantage of the system is that it dispenses with the carrying of cash which is fully negotiable of course and once transferred by a thief to an innocent transferee for value is completely lost even though it might be traced. The cheque book has replaced the wallet. The cheque backed by the bankers card has replaced cash.

Credit cards

For most of this century we have been accustomed to credit extended by shops. The poor man bought his food and often his clothes 'on tick', paying some of the debt if not all, when his wages were received. The better-off classes, shopping at fashionable departmental stores, still expected credit in exactly the same way, paying the store when salary day came round. Large stores encouraged it by offering credit customers small discounts since they prospered on customer loyalty. The customer's loyalty with many people arose so often through the absence of cash that might have enabled shopping elsewhere to have taken place. Such credit customers were (and still are) given a 'card' bearing the specimen signature of the customer to enable him to move from department to department and effect his (her) purchases with consumate ease. The store has always sent a monthly statement to the customer and expects the debt to be cleared some time during the month following the purchases. Thus a new coat bought on 2 April was often paid for on 29 May, a credit period of nearly two months.

If we enlarge the model to the whole country and make each department a separate retail outlet, we have almost an identical situation. Instead of the departmental store company we have the credit-card company to which thousands of wholesalers and retailers look to for payment when selling goods to credit-card holders. Just as the department store allowed, say, 5 per cent discount to credit customers, now the sellers of goods and services are prepared to pay a small percentage of the sale proceeds to the credit-card company. Many retailers support the credit-card schemes since they know that as soon as the buyer has signed the cash-sales form provided by the credit-card company, it is as good as cash. Such forms are paid into a bank for collection in almost the identical way with cheques. Such forms are not transferable and in no way can they be said to equate a cheque though they are claims to money owing to the retailer by the credit-card company. Just as the departmental store sent statements to credit customers (and no doubt still do) for settlement during the month following the purchases, so does the credit-card company. Both charge interest on the amount not cleared; in fact it might appear that the credit-card company (associated with a commercial bank normally) encourages such delays in payment since the rate of interest charged on the outstanding unpaid balance is relatively high.

The credit card itself bears embossed details of the card holder together with his specimen signature and the seller uses a small machine to transfer the embossed details to the sales form, the claim against the credit card company. If the card falls into wrong hands then its misuse is obvious since with a simple bit of forgery one can go shopping to one's heart's content and the loss will fall on the credit-card company unless they can show that the card holder was very dilatory in reporting the loss after such loss was discovered. If the loss of a card is quickly reported then such loss can be recorded at the computer. Large retailers with computer terminals can very quickly check to see if a card tendered to them is in wrong hands.

This card, unlike the bankers card, reduces the need for a large number of cheques since the whole of one's purchases for a month can be paid for with one single cheque. The card is of no value, it is not transferable and cannot in any circumstances be associated with a negotiable instrument. It is, what its name clearly implies, a means of shopping on credit. The account held by the credit-card-holder is a credit account relating to a series of purchases, whereas the bankers card is associated entirely with a bank current account.

Index